# Theory of Music

Richard T. Dasher

J. WESTON
WALCH
PUBLISHER

PORTLAND, MAINE

1  2  3  4  5  6  7  8  9  10

ISBN 0-8251-2469-7

Copyright © 1994
J. Weston Walch, Publisher
P. O. Box 658 • Portland, Maine 04104-0658

Printed in the United States of America

# Contents

# Introduction

Learning to write music is a bit like learning to write a language you already speak. Chances are, you are already a *performer* of music—a singer or an instrumentalist. You may already be skillful at reading notation, and have some information about how to write music. But your present impression may be somewhat disorganized or inaccurate. In the language of music, your vocabulary is good, but your grammar needs some polishing.

Whether you are arranging someone else's music or writing your own, you will want your work to sound as professional as possible. The principles of musical grammar were developed over hundreds of years, through experimentation by some of the world's finest musicians. Even when musicians "break" the conventions of music, they know what they are doing, and they do it only for a special reason.

We are concerned here with musical grammar (more properly, musical *syntax*), and with learning how to write smooth, effective music of many types. The principles of musical grammar are not absolute; they may be avoided when it suits the musician's expressive purposes. They were compiled in instruction manuals, many of which were written almost three centuries ago by a French musician named Rameau. They have been used by professional composers ever since, even though musicians expand or even ignore them at times. Almost all the music you hear today is based on the fundamental principles that Rameau codified so long ago. Jazz and pop, country and rock, classical and blues—all share a harmonic vocabulary and a syntax that we will explore in this book.

Hearing the music *you* wrote is a marvelous thrill, and I hope you can do it often. Music is, after all, sounds in the air, not notes on a page. You want to get to the "air" stage as often and as directly as possible. On the other hand, try not to fall in love with your first efforts. At this stage, you are making experiments, not creating deathless art. Be critical of your own work, and of the work of others. Most pencils have erasers, and both ends of your pencil should be used judiciously.

There is no guarantee that by following all the principles you will write great music; nor can I guarantee that you will never write great music *unless* you follow the principles. Chances are, however, that the more careful you are with musical syntax, the better your music will sound—and that's what writing music is all about. You'll need a lot of manuscript paper, and don't be stingy with it. Try things, change things, throw away your old scratch copy, and leave room for corrections and alterations. Always make neat, clean copies of your products for performance; other people must read your manuscript, and you want your efforts to sound as good as they really are.

Two brief comments before we begin. First, it is *most* important that you sharpen your skills of music reading and train your ear to hear more acutely. You *must* sight-sing regularly, and you *must* practice listening to music and analyzing it. Second, you learn to write music only by writing it. Some of what you write won't please you, but you must keep on writing to get any better. Don't sit around waiting for inspiration to strike, take pencil in hand and go at it. If one idea doesn't work out, try again until something does. Once you start writing, the ideas will come. Then, find a way to *hear* your own work; it's exciting, it's interesting, and it makes all music mean much more to you.

All set? Then let's begin.

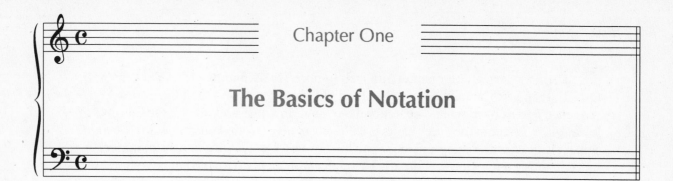

## Chapter One

# The Basics of Notation

Music is sound. When we speak of "writing music," what we mean is "writing symbols that represent musical sounds." When you become involved in the mechanics of writing music, you may forget to try the results in performance from time to time. What looks good on paper will not necessarily sound good when it is performed. So, as a final test, you must perform everything you write.

Writing symbols for music involves representing at least three elements of sound: *pitch* (how high or low a tone is), *duration* (how long or short a tone is), and *dynamic* (how loud or soft a tone is). There are standard ways of representing each of these elements. In this chapter, we will survey these standard symbols, many of which you probably already know. You should read through this chapter carefully, however, since it is the cornerstone on which the rest of this book is built.

## The Staff

Pitch is represented by the placement of notes on a series of lines and spaces called a *staff*. Each note is placed either on a line (that is, with the line going through the middle of the note, ) or in a space (that is, at a location midway between two lines, ). The basic staff on which notes are written consists of eleven lines. It is called the *grand staff*. This is the staff on which piano music is usually written. The top five lines are indicated by a *treble clef*, ; the bottom five lines are indicated by a *bass clef*, . To simplify the task of reading music written on the grand staff, the middle line of the eleven is normally *not* written in unless a note is to appear on that line. The short line that is used for this note is called a *ledger line*, and the note written on this middle line is called *middle C*.

The easiest way to comprehend the grand staff is to relate the notes to the keys of a piano. The middle C of the staff is the C nearest the center of the piano keyboard. One might expect the middle note of the staff to be called A rather than C. If we were to set about inventing the staff today, we might adopt such a sensible arrangement. However, the present staff has been in existence for more than a thousand years, so its form, though perhaps not entirely logical, is unlikely to be changed.

There are seven letter names attached to notes. In ascending order, they are A, B, C, D, E, F, and G. The next note higher than G is another A, and then the entire sequence begins over again. The interval between one note and the next higher or lower one with the same letter name is called an *octave* (from the Latin word for *eight*, since it is the eighth scale step above the lower one). Octaves are of special importance in music and in musical theory. This is because any two tones that have the same letter name blend so perfectly together in sound that they give no feeling of being different tones. Try this on the piano: play any two C's, or A's, or D's at the same time, and listen carefully to the result. Now play any two tones with different letter names (such as A and B, or C and F, or G and E) at the same time. Compare the effect. In these latter examples, there are unmistakably two notes sounding. This is why all octaves bear the same letter name.

Notes on the staff, then, go upward in seven-note sequences from the bottom line of the bass staff (G) to the top line of the treble staff (F). They go beyond the staff as well, both above and below, using ledger lines as needed above and below the grand staff. They are always named in the same sequence. Study the staff and keyboard below to see how this system works. Remember that each note on the staff refers to a particular key on the keyboard. That is, middle C is always the C closest to the center of the keyboard; the C in the third space up, on the treble staff, is always the C one octave above middle C; and so on. Illustration 1 shows the grand staff, labeled with

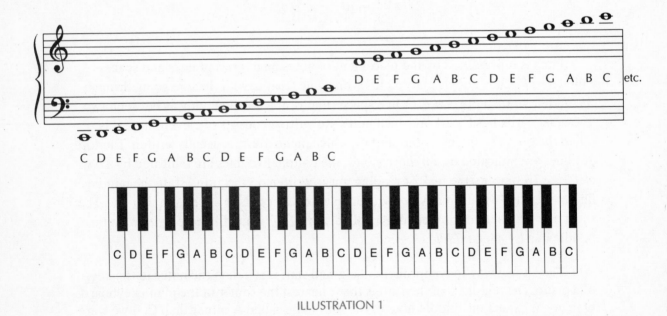

ILLUSTRATION 1

the letter names of the notes that appear on the lines and spaces. After you have studied this material carefully, you are ready to test your knowledge with Worksheet #1.

## Measures, Bar Lines, and Double Bar Lines

Music is an art that exists in time, not in space. Paintings, sculptures, or buildings can be measured in feet, meters, or pounds; music is measured in beats, or counts per minute. Written notes indicate how many beats (or fractions of a beat) a given tone is to be held for. *Measures*, in turn, mark off the staff into even segments of so many beats each. Each measure ends in a *bar line*—a single vertical line crossing a staff. At the end of a major section of a composition, and again at the end of the whole composition, a *double bar line* is used to signify an ending. Find all these elements in Illustration 2.

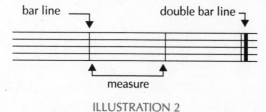

ILLUSTRATION 2

We can use the analogy of a ruler, with inches representing beats of music. We can subdivide four inches in a number of ways: by whole inches, by half inches, or by quarter or eighth inches, for example. The four-inch length will always remain the same distance, however, and all the subdivisions must add up to the full four inches. Each measure constitutes a certain number of musical "inches" and is only complete when the subdivisions add up to the full measure.

## Meter Signatures, Notes, and Rests

In written music, each measure is filled with notes, rests, or combinations of the two. Each note or rest is held by the performer for a specific number of beats or fractions of a beat. The total amount of notes and rests in any given measure is determined by the *meter signature*.

At the very beginning of a line of music, shortly after the clef, is a meter signature (or "time signature"). In most cases, this consists of two numbers, one above the other in this fashion: $\frac{4}{4}$ . Written in this way, a meter signature resembles a fraction, but it is not. Each number conveys certain information about the notes in the following measures.

*The top number indicates the number of beats in each measure.* This number could conceivably be any whole number—1, 2, 3, 4, 5, 9, 11, 15, or any other. (Some modern composers even use whole numbers and fractions, for example $\frac{5\frac{1}{2}}{4}$ !) The top number is usually **2**, **3**, or **4** ; the numbers **6**, **9**, and **12** are less common; **5**, **7**, **11**, and others are rarities.

*The bottom number identifies the type of note that lasts for one beat.* For example, the number 𝟦 on the bottom indicates that the quarter note gets one beat (see discussion of note values, below). *All other notes take their values from this one.* The half note, for example, which is twice as long as the quarter note, is held for two beats; the eighth note, which is half the duration of the quarter note, lasts for half a beat; and so on.

The basic type of note is the *whole note* ○ , which gets its name from the fact that it fills an entire measure in what is called "common time" ( $\frac{4}{4}$ meter). The *half note* ♩ (♪) resembles the whole note, but has a stem attached to one side. The half note is held for two beats in common time; that is, half the length of a whole note.

The *quarter note* ♩ (♩) has the form of a half note with the note's head filled in. It is held for one fourth the time of a whole note, or one beat in $\frac{4}{4}$ meter. The *eighth note* resembles a quarter note with a *flag* ♪ (♪), and is held for one eighth the time of a whole note (one-half beat in common time). When two or more notes with flags are written in succession, the flags are often joined together into a *beam* ♫ (♫). All other basic notes are formed by adding more flags, and each is half as long in duration as the one with one less flag.

Suppose, now, that we have a meter signature of $\frac{4}{2}$ . This would mean that the half note (𝟤) would be held for one beat, the whole note for two, the quarter note for one half, and so on. In $\frac{6}{8}$ time, on the other hand, the eighth note (𝟪) would be held for one count, the quarter note for two, the sixteenth note for half a count, and so on. Thus, the bottom number of a meter signature must be 1, 2, 4, 8, 16, or some other number in geometric progression from that point. Illustration 3 clarifies which numbers may be on the bottom of a meter signature, and which note each number assigns the duration of one count.

| Bottom number | Type of note |
|:---:|:---:|
| 1 | ○ |
| 2 | ♩ |
| 4 | ♩ |
| 8 | ♪ |
| 16 | ♬ |

ILLUSTRATION 3

Undoubtedly there is a better way to indicate the sort of note that is to receive one count. It would be much more sensible to write meter signatures as $\frac{4}{\bullet}$ or $\frac{6}{\flat}$, so that there would be no confusion about which note lasts for how long. Nonetheless, most music is written with two-numeral meter signatures, so we must learn how to interpret them. "Tradition" is also the reason we don't simply say, "A quarter note *always* lasts for a beat, a half *always* lasts for two beats," and so on. If publishers were suddenly to make such an assertion, a vast amount of music in $\frac{2}{2}$ or $\frac{6}{8}$ or some other meter would have to be copied over, or "translated" into the proper notation. It is much easier to teach each new generation to be flexible about reading notes!

Tradition also keeps alive two non-numerical meter signatures. The first of these, $\mathbf{C}$, stands for $\frac{4}{4}$, or "common time." It looks like a large letter C for "common," but it actually represents a broken circle. Centuries ago, music was closely related to religion. Music with three beats per measure was considered to be in "perfect" meter because the number three represents the Christian Trinity. Such musical meter was symbolized by a circle, a Christian symbol for perfection, because a circle has no beginning or end. Music in two or four beats per measure, therefore, was considered to be in an imperfect meter, and was symbolized by a broken circle. The second non-numerical meter signature is called "cut time," $\mathbf{\mathcal{C}}$, and represents $\frac{4}{4}$ time cut in half, or $\frac{2}{2}$ meter.

The best way to visualize these different meter signatures is to see the same melody written in various meters. Remember that all three of these versions will sound *exactly the same* if played at the same basic speed.

"Yankee Doodle"

ILLUSTRATION 4

For each note, there exists a *rest* of equivalent length. Rests are not passive moments when one has nothing to do; rather, they are *silences* of specific duration that the composer has written. They must be counted as carefully as the notes.

The *whole rest* ⏤ corresponds in duration to the whole note; that is, it is held for four counts in common time. The *half rest* ⏤, half the duration of a whole rest, looks confusingly similar. One way to differentiate between them is to imagine the whole rest, the longer one, as being heavier than the half rest; the whole rest hangs *below* the line, while the lighter half rest sits *on* the line.

The *quarter rest* 𝄽 is held for one count in common time. The *eighth rest* 𝄾 looks a bit like a stylized "7," and it lasts as long as an eighth note. *Sixteenth rests* 𝄿 and *thirty-second rests* 𝄿 add "tails" in exactly the same way their corresponding notes add flags. For reference, here is a chart of notes and their equivalent rests:

| # of beats | Note | Rest |
|:---:|:---:|:---:|
| 4 | o | ⏤ |
| 2 | ♩ | ⏤ |
| 1 | ♩ | 𝄽 |
| 1/2 | ♪ | 𝄾 |
| 1/4 | ♬ | 𝄿 |
| 1/8 | ♬ | 𝄿 |

ILLUSTRATION 5

(All values assume 4/4 meter.)

Each of these notes and rests may be extended, or made longer, by adding a dot after the note. The dot extends the note by half its original length; the note then becomes longer than its undotted form. Thus, in $\frac{6}{4}$ time, a dotted whole note is held for six counts: four for the note, plus half of four (two) for the dot, totaling six. A dotted half note is held for three counts: two plus half of two (one), totaling three. The same principle applies not only to the other notes, but all the rests as well. This is shown in Illustration 6.

| # of beats | Note | Rest |
|:---:|:---:|:---:|
| 6 | o· | ⏤· |

*(continued)*

| # of beats | Note | Rest |
|:---:|:---:|:---:|
| 3 | 𝅗𝅥. | ▬▪. |
| 1 1/2 | ♩. | 𝄾. |
| 3/4 | ♪. | 𝄿. |
| 3/8 | 𝅘𝅥𝅯. | 𝄿. |
| 3/16 | 𝅘𝅥𝅰. | 𝄿. |

ILLUSTRATION 6
(All values assume 6/4 meter.)

If you feel you have mastered the above information, you are ready to do Worksheet #2. Have your teacher check over your work.

## Accidentals: Sharps, Flats, and Naturals

So far we have directed our attention to only the white keys of the piano. The black keys are of equal importance, but they take their names from adjacent white keys. Notice, for example, that there is a black key between each C and each D. The pitch of this key is somewhat higher than C but not as high as D. Play these keys on the piano so that you can hear the difference. Any note that is a bit higher than another, but not high enough to have the next letter name, is referred to as the *sharp* version of the lower tone. Thus, in relation to C, this black key is called C-sharp.

Notice that the black keys fall into a repeating pattern of groups of two and three keys, moving from left to right of C. (Refer to the keyboard in Illustration 1.) The lower (that is, the farther left) of the two black keys is always C-sharp; the higher of the two is always D-sharp. The next black key to the right (the lowest of the group of three) is adjacent to the white key F; therefore, that black key is F-sharp, the middle black key is G-sharp, and the highest is A-sharp. To state a rule for finding sharps, then, *the sharp of a white key is always the next key to the right.*

However, these same black keys may be viewed in another light; that is, by looking at the white keys to the right of the black keys. Let's go back to our C-sharp and consider it in relation to D, the white key to its right. Any note that is a bit lower than another, but not low enough to have the next letter name, is called the *flat* version of the higher note. Thus, in relation to the note D, the farther left of the two black keys is called D-flat 🎼. *The flat of a white key is always the next key to its left.* Thus, each black key always bears two names: one as a sharp and the other as a flat. C-sharp is the same key as D-flat; D-sharp is E-flat; F-sharp is G-flat; G-sharp is A-flat; and A-sharp is B-flat. At the moment, this all probably seems needlessly complex; why have *two* names for each black key? Couldn't we always refer to each as C-sharp or F-sharp, and disregard the flatted versions? The answer, of course, is no. As to why this is so, we must leave the answer for another chapter, when we discuss various types of scales.

Since there are seven white keys but only five black keys, two of the white keys must also serve as flats or sharps. The note E has no black key immediately to its right, so F serves as E-sharp when necessary. C serves as B-sharp in the same fashion. E and B return the favor to F and C by serving as F-flat and C-flat from time to time. Thus, the rules originally stated still hold, even in the absence of black keys: *The next key to the right (left) of any white key is the sharp (flat) of that key.*

Sometimes in music one needs to use a flat or sharp and then use the unaltered note shortly thereafter. This is accomplished by using the *natural sign* ♮. Illustration 7 shows some ways in which this sign can be used. The natural sign indicates that the

ILLUSTRATION 7

normal white key for that note is to be played. By convention, an *accidental* (a sharp, flat, or natural introduced in a measure) lasts *only* for the measure in which it appears; the bar line "cancels" the accidental. This is not true of key signatures.

## Dynamic Markings

Intensity of sound is indicated by combinations of three Italian words or their initial letters. These words are *forte* (strong, rather than loud), *piano* (soft), and *mezzo* (moderately). Thus, a part marked *p* (for *piano*) is to be played softly; a part marked *mp* (for *mezzo piano*) would be played slightly louder; and so on. For very soft or very strong, the initial letters are doubled—*pp* or *ff*. The Italian words used here are *pianissimo* and *fortissimo*. On occasion, even more *p*'s or *f*'s are used. For example, *fff* would be termed *fortississimo*. The ultimate expression of such dynamic overkill appears in the first movement of Tchaikovsky's Sixth Symphony, in which a solo clarinet part is marked *ppppp—pianississississimo*. Incidentally, the very next chord is marked *ff*.

The most common dynamic markings are the following:

| *pp* | *pianissimo* | very softly |
| --- | --- | --- |
| *p* | *piano* | softly |
| *mp* | *mezzo piano* | moderately softly |
| *mf* | *mezzo forte* | moderately strongly |
| *f* | *forte* | strongly |
| *ff* | *fortissimo* | very strongly |

Changes in dynamics are indicated in a number of ways. If the change is to take place over a relatively few notes or measures, it will be represented pictorially. The symbol  ⟨  indicates that the tone is to get gradually louder; its reverse,  ⟩, indicates that the tone should get gradually softer. If the change is to be made over a longer span of measures, the words *crescendo* (becoming louder) or *diminuendo* (becoming softer) may be used. These may be abbreviated *cresc.* or *dim.* Usually, the new dynamic level to be arrived at is also indicated, for example, *dim........p*, or *cresc.......ff*.

## Other Musical Symbols

There are thousands of symbols and terms used in music; we will describe only the most common ones here. You should have access to a good musical dictionary or encyclopedia such as the *Harvard Dictionary of Music*, by Don Randel, or the *New College Encyclopedia of Music*, by Westrup and Harrison. Certain marks are so common, however, that we should describe them here.

Curved lines ♩♪ are often placed above or below notes. Such lines are of two general types: ties and slurs. *Ties* connect two notes of the *same* pitch, as shown here.

ILLUSTRATION 8

They indicate that the pitch being played or sung is to be continued for the combined length of the tied-together notes. In the first example in Illustration 8, the pitch would be held for three counts; in the second, the pitch would be held for one and three-fourths counts. *Slurs* connect notes with *different* pitches. They indicate that the performer is to move smoothly from one pitch to another, with no separation between pitches, as shown here.

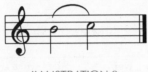

ILLUSTRATION 9

*Accents* are of various types. The most common is the v-on-its-side accent $>$, which instructs the performer to emphasize the note below (or sometimes above) by striking or tonguing harder than usual, or by singing or bowing louder. The inverted-v accent $\Lambda$ tells the performer to emphasize and to shorten the note a bit. Sometimes a heavy accent is indicated by the word *sforzando*, or by its abbreviation *sfz*.

Some notes have a dot above or below them and are to be played short and spaced; this symbol is called *staccato* . Its opposite, *tenuto*, is indicated by a dash above or below the note . That note is then held out for full value and played smoothly.

The *repeat sign* appears in two types of circumstances. The *repeat sign* is a double bar with two dots placed just before it:

ILLUSTRATION 10A

This sign instructs you to repeat the entire previous section. If the sign appears early in the piece, you are to return to the very beginning and play the whole section through a second time.

If the repeated section is in the middle or toward the end of a piece, it will be set off by a reversed phrase repeat sign:

ILLUSTRATION 10B

This symbol tells you where to begin the repeat. Sometimes the repeated section is to be ended differently the second time; in such a case, *first and second endings* of one or more measures are used. They look like this:

ILLUSTRATION 11

While the above symbols instruct the performer to repeat the entire passage before, there is another common symbol that indicates the previous measure should be played again, exactly as written. This is the *measure repeat sign*, and it looks like this:

ILLUSTRATION 12

Several Italian words indicate changes in speed. *Accelerando* (*accel.*) means to gradually become faster. *Allargando* (*allarg.*) and/or *ritardando* (*rit.*) mean to gradually become slower. There are many terms to describe the manner in which a piece is to be performed, such as *dolce* (sweetly), *leggiero* (lightly), and *con anima* (with spirit). Consult a musical dictionary for definitions of words you don't understand.

Other words indicate the overall speed, or *tempo*, at which a piece should be played. The following table gives the words and the speeds, in beats per minute, that they indicate. Use a metronome to hear how slow or fast these speeds are.

| Term | Speed (beats per minute) |
|---|---|
| *Grave* | 40–42 |
| *Largo* | 44–46 |
| *Lento* | 48–50 |
| *Adagio* | 54–58 |
| *Larghetto* | 60–69 |
| *Andante* | 72–76 |
| *Andantino* | 80–84 |
| *Moderato* | 88–96 |
| *Allegretto* | 100–116 |
| *Allegro* | 120–138 |
| *Allegro assai* | 144 |
| *Allegro vivace* | 152 |

| Term | Speed (beats per minute) |
|---|---|
| *Vivace* | 160–168 |
| *Presto* | 176–192 |
| *Prestissimo* | 200–208 |

It is not necessary for you to memorize this list of tempos, as long as you have a table like it to refer to when you need it.

One other common symbol is the *fermata*, or "bird's-eye" ⌒. This sign indicates that the note or rest below it is to be held for an indefinite time, until the performer or conductor decides to go ahead. The note should be held for at least twice its normal value.

If you feel you have mastered the material at the end of this chapter, you may proceed to Worksheet #3. As always, have your teacher go over your work to ensure that you understand it.

1. How many lines are there on a *grand staff*? _____

2. What symbol tells you that the *top* five lines are being used? _____

3. How many lines are there in a *treble staff*? _____

4. What symbol indicates that the *bottom* five lines are being used? _____

5. Define a ledger line: _____

   _____

   _____

6. The distance from any note to the next higher or lower note with the same letter

   name is called an _____.

7. What are the seven letter names used in music?_____

   _____

8. Give the letter names of these notes:

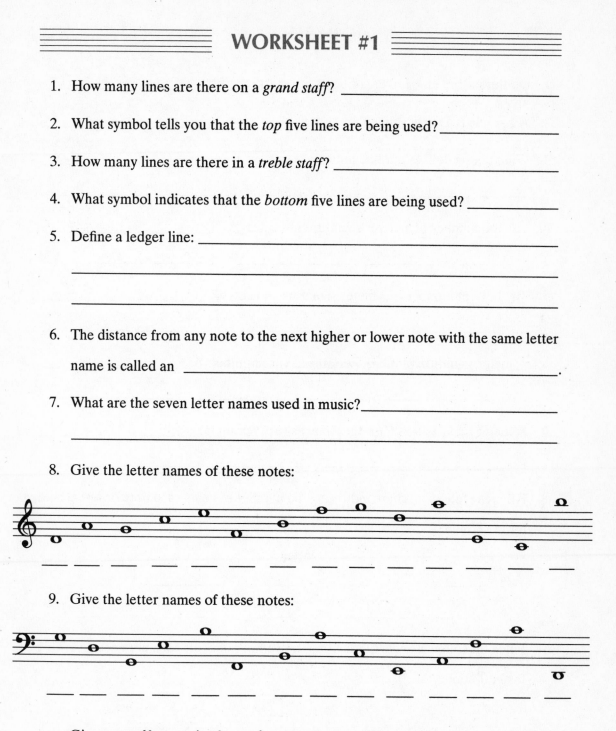

9. Give the letter names of these notes:

   Give yourself one point for each correct answer. Have your teacher go over your
worksheet to clarify any problems you have. Stay with this level until you understand
the material perfectly.

# WORKSHEET #2

1. On the staff, even numbers of beats are marked off by _____.

2. A bar line is a vertical line that ends a _____.

3. What does a double bar line indicate? _____

   _____

4. The top number of a meter signature indicates_____

   _____.

5. The bottom number of a meter signature indicates _____

   _____.

6. A meter signature of **C** is the same as (use numbers) _____

   _____.

7. A meter signature of **¢** is the same as (use numbers) _____

   _____.

8. Fill in the following chart, indicating the number of beats each note or rest is held

   for in $\frac{4}{4}$ time.

9. Fill in the following chart, indicating the number of beats each note or rest is held

   for in $\frac{6}{8}$ time.

10. Fill in the following chart, indicating the number of beats each note or rest is held for in $\frac{2}{2}$ time.

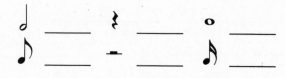

11. When a note or rest is followed by a dot, the note or rest _____

_____.

Give yourself one point for each correct answer. Have your teacher go over your worksheet to clarify any problems you have. Stay with this level until you understand the material perfectly.

# WORKSHEET #3

1. Once an accidental is introduced, for how long is it in effect? _____

   _____

2. What effect does a natural sign have? _____

   _____

3. For each of the following abbreviations, write out the complete Italian term and the English version:

   a. *pp* _____

   b. *p* _____

   c. *mp* _____

   d. *mf* _____

   e. *f* _____

   f. *ff* _____

4. Define each of the following Italian terms as they apply to music:

   a. *crescendo* _____

   b. *diminuendo* _____

   c. *accelerando* _____

   d. *allargando*, or *ritardando* _____

   e. *fermata* [⌒] _____

5. For each of the following pairs of terms, indicate which is faster, a or b, by circling the appropriate letter.

   | a. *adagio* | b. *allegro* |
   |---|---|
   | a. *vivace* | b. *lento* |
   | a. *presto* | b. *andante* |
   | a. *moderato* | b. *allegretto* |
   | a. *andantino* | b. *larghetto* |

6. Name each of the following symbols:

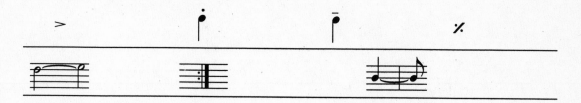

Give yourself one point for each correct answer. Have your teacher go over your worksheet to clarify any problems you have.

## Chapter Two

# Writing Music Notation

From this point onward in your study of music theory, you will be called on to do many exercises in manuscript. Printed notation is clear, neat, precise, and very time-consuming to imitate by hand. It is extremely important that your manuscript be as clear and precise as possible, so that it can be read accurately by a performer. As with any form of penmanship, it will take time and much practice for you to develop a neat, clear manuscript "style." The following suggestions will aid you in your writing. Always use a No. 2 lead pencil for your writing, and *always* be prepared to erase!

## Clef Signs

The treble and bass clefs are used most commonly in music writing. Another form of clef, the C clef ( $\mathfrak{k}$ ), is used in writing music for certain instruments; it will not be used in this book. The treble clef, often called the G clef, indicates the line on which the note G above middle C will be written. The last little curl on the clef intersects the G line of the staff:

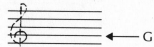

The treble clef is usually drawn in four steps. In Step 1, a vertical line is drawn, extending slightly above and below the five-line staff:

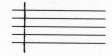

In Step 2, a small loop is drawn at the top and to the right of the vertical line. This loop should rejoin the vertical line at the fourth line of the staff (all lines and spaces are counted from the bottom upward; the fourth line is fourth from the bottom):

In Step 3, a larger loop is drawn to the left of the vertical line, extending from the fourth to the bottom line:

In Step 4, the final curlicue is added; this configuration cuts across the second line twice:

The whole figure is usually drawn in two strokes, the vertical stroke first and then the series of loops in one continuous motion. Draw them very carefully until you can get the hang of drawing the figure.

The bass clef, also known as the F clef, locates F below middle C on the fourth line of the staff. The bass clef can be drawn in two steps. In Step 1, a large, looping curve is drawn beginning just below the fourth line, rising to the fifth line, and swinging downward to the right to end just below the second line:

In Step 2, two dots are placed to the right of the clef, bracketing the fourth line. The clef is now complete:

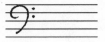

# Notes

Writing notes requires consideration of at least three elements: note heads, stems, and flags or beams. We shall consider each of these elements separately.

## Note Heads

The first essential is that the note heads be clearly either on a *line* (—●—) or in a *space* ( ⊃●⊂ ). It will help if you make the heads oval in shape rather than circular, and definitely not too large. A whole note can be made in one stroke, —⊖— or ⊃○⊂ . Filled-in note heads (for instance, quarter or eighth notes) can be a bit smaller. Draw the oval first, then color it in:  —●— or ⊃●⊂ .

## *Stems*

Stems are attached to the side of the note, and they should be about three lines or spaces tall. If a note head is on a line, the stem should extend three lines above or below it, or the equivalent distance; if the head is in a space, the stem should extend three spaces above or below:

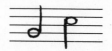

Stems are drawn to the *right* of the note if the stems go upward, and to the *left* of the note if they go downward. All notes below the middle line have upward stems; all notes above the middle line have downward stems. Notes *on* the middle line may have stems in either direction. Usually, if the other notes in the measure have upward stems, so will the note on the middle line, and vice versa:

middle line ⟶

It is not necessary for stems to actually connect with their note heads. They should come very close, but for the sake of swifter writing it is permissible to have a small gap: ♩ ⌐ ♩ ⌐ . Be sure to space your note heads so that your measure is not too crowded; about an eighth of an inch, or more, between note heads is a good separation. If a note is dotted, you must allow extra space for the dot: ♩. ♪. . If two or more notes are to be played at the same time, they must be placed one *exactly over* the other:

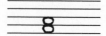

## *Flags and Beams*

Flags are always placed to the right of a stem. If the stem goes upward, a flag is simply a curved line coming down from the top: ♪. If the stem goes downward, the flag comes upward from the bottom of the stem: ⌐ . Eighth notes are usually made in three steps: first the head ( • ); then the stem, drawn with a downward stroke ( ⌐ or ♩ ); and finally, the flag, again drawn with a downward stroke ( ⌐ or ♪ ). Multiple flags, used for sixteenth or thirty-second notes, are similarly drawn, one flag per stroke, with the ends joined together ( ♬ ).

When two flagged notes appear in succession, they will often be joined by a beam, rather than be given separate flags: ♫ rather than ♪♪. Again, beams may appear above the note heads ♫ or below them ♫. Try to make the beams a bit heavier then the stems, especially if the beam follows a line:

When there is a dotted eighth-note and sixteenth-note combination connected by a beam, the sixteenth note is indicated by a short extra beam to the *left* of the stem: ♫ or ♫. When beamed notes go up or down on the staff, the beam slopes to connect the tops of the stems: ♫ ♫. Examine printed music to see other ways of treating beamed notes.

## Bar Lines, Double Bar Lines, and Repeats

When music is written on a single staff, bar lines are simply single vertical lines extending from the bottom line to the top. When two or more staves are to be played together, as in a grand staff, the bar lines connect the two staves.

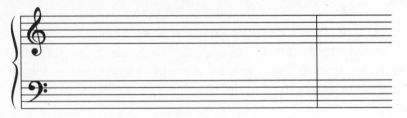

Double bars are usually written with the second bar somewhat thicker than the first:

A repeat sign is made up of a thin line with a thicker line on its outside and two dots on its inside (that is, the side of the section to be repeated):

Make your dots very distinct, always surrounding the middle line. Measures at the end of a line should always be complete measures; don't begin them on one line and complete them on the next. If you have some unused staff after the last full measure on a line, scribble it out so that someone reading the line won't be confused by the blank staff.

## Rests

Rests are always placed in the middle of the staff. A whole rest is a small, filled-in rectangle suspended from the fourth line:

Whole rests are sometimes used to indicate a silent measure in $\frac{3}{4}$ or even $\frac{2}{4}$ time. When so used, they indicate three (or two) beats of silence, rather than four beats. Half rests are similar rectangles set on the third line:

Each rectangle should fill about half the space between lines 3 and 4.

When several measures in any meter are silent, it may be indicated in a different manner. A longer, heavy bar is drawn over the third line, with short vertical lines at either end, and a numeral indicating the number of measures of rest that are represented:

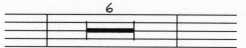

Draw the heavy bar first, add the short lines, and then place the numeral above the staff, centered over the rest.

The quarter rest is a cumbersome symbol. It can be drawn in four steps. In Step 1, draw a short diagonal line sloping downward to the right, beginning in the fourth space and extending to the third space:

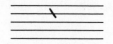

In Step 2, a short diagonal line is drawn from the bottom of the first diagonal line to the left. It should reach approximately the third line of the staff:

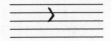

In Step 3, another short diagonal line to the right is drawn, this time extending to about the middle of the second space:

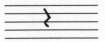

Finally, in Step 4, a swooping, left-to-right downward curve is drawn from the end of Step 3, reaching the bottom line of the staff:

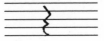

The eighth rest is easily drawn in two steps. In Step 1, draw a short upward curve, extending from the third to the fourth space of the staff:

In Step 2, draw a downward diagonal to the left from the top of Step 1, ending on the second line of the staff:

For sixteenth or thirty-second rests, use the same pattern, but add flags as necessary:

## Meter Signatures

The meter signature is placed just after the clef and the key signature at the beginning of the staff. When numerals are used, the top numeral should fit in the top two spaces, and the bottom numeral should fit in the bottom two spaces:

When C or ₵ is used, the figure should extend from the second to the fourth lines; the vertical line for ₵ should extend from the first to the fourth space:

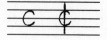

## Sharps, Flats, and Naturals

You must take the same care to center these symbols on a line or in a space that you use when placing note heads. The square box of the sharp should be exactly on a line or in a space:

The same is true for the parallelogram that forms the center of the natural:

Sharps are made like a tic-tac-toe board; that is, two strokes down ‖ followed by two strokes across ♯ that are slanted slightly upward. Naturals are made by the "L7" method: first drawn an L with its horizontal leg tilted upwards L ; then draw a 7 with the crossbar also slanted and attached to the L ♮ . The flat is a bit less precise in placement, but the space in the center of the flat should be clearly either on a line or in a space:

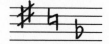

The vertical lines of all three figures should be about two lines or spaces long:

When these accidentals are used beside a note, they *always* appear to the left of the note. Remember to leave extra space for them:

When writing key signatures (which come immediately after the clef), you may allow less than one eighth of an inch between each sharp or flat. Be sure to place them in the correct order, from left to right.

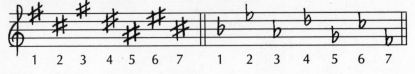

Finally, do not be afraid to rewrite your manuscript. Do your practice work on one scratch sheet, but hand in your final copy as neatly done as you can manage. This self-discipline will pay off handsomely later on. Have fun, and happy manuscripting!

## Chapter Three

# Scales

In the music with which you are most familiar, the individual notes are arranged in patterns called *scales*. The term comes from the Italian word *scala*, meaning "ladder." A scale, then, is a ladder of notes used to go higher and lower. There are two main characteristics of scales: first, their notes are arranged in order, either ascending or descending; second, the lowest tone of the scale is the "home tone" and is more important than the rest, for reasons we will get to shortly. There are many different types of scales, some of which we'll meet later in this book; but for now we'll concentrate on *major scales*.

## Whole and Half Steps

A major scale is one member of the family of *diatonic scales*. A diatonic scale uses two sizes of steps, whole steps and half steps. We can best illustrate this by playing the white keys on a piano from any C to the C an octave higher; this automatically gives us a major scale. The pattern of white and black keys on the piano keyboard is so important that you must memorize it and be able to draw it accurately from memory. If you haven't already done so, study Illustration 1 now until you know exactly where the white and black keys appear.

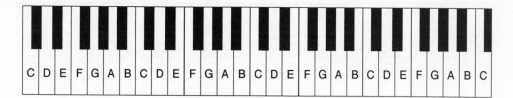

ILLUSTRATION 1

From this illustration of a keyboard, you can see that in between C and D there is a black key (C-sharp or D-flat). Since there is a half-step distance between any two adjacent keys on the piano, the distance from C to the nearest black key (C-sharp) is a half step. The distance from C-sharp to D is also a half step. The distance from C to D, then, is a whole step (C to C-sharp is one half-step; C-sharp to D is a second half step).

The same holds true for the distance from D to E. This is also a whole step because there is a black key between them.

Now look at the distance from E to F. Here we have *no* black key between them, so the distance is only a half step. From F to G is a whole step, from G to A is a whole step, and from A to B is a whole step, but from B to C is only a half step, since there is no black key between these white keys. Thus, by playing the white keys from C to C we get the distances (or *intervals*) given in Illustration 2. This pattern of whole and half steps makes up what we call a major scale

ILLUSTRATION 2

## Using Flats and Sharps

Keep in mind that it is this *pattern* that makes a major scale, no matter what note you start on as the home tone. Another way to think of this is to recall the singing syllables: *do, re, mi, fa, sol, la, ti,* and *do.* (We often use the letters *d, r, m, f, s, l,* and *t* to represent these syllables.) Any note may be *do,* but the distance from *do* to *re* will always be a whole step, from *re* to *mi* will be a whole step, from *mi* to *fa* will be a half step, and so forth. Of course, in order to keep the pattern the same, it may be necessary to use some or all of the black keys. For example, if we call F *do,* instead of C, and if we apply the same pattern of whole and half steps, we must lower the fourth note (B) by a half step, making it B-flat. Similarly, if we call G *do,* we must raise the seventh note (F) to F-sharp, as in Illustration 3. Play these scales on a piano or some other

ILLUSTRATION 3

instrument, first with the original notes and then with the changed notes, and listen to the differences the changed notes make.

Some scales require two or more (up to seven) sharps or flats to make the pattern work out correctly. Illustration 4 shows all the major scales that are in common use. Notice that the scales of C-sharp and D-flat, although they are written differently, use the same pitches. The same is true of two other pairs of scales— F-sharp and G-flat, and B and C-flat. While there are fifteen *written* scales, there are only twelve different *sound* scales, one for each black or white key in an octave.

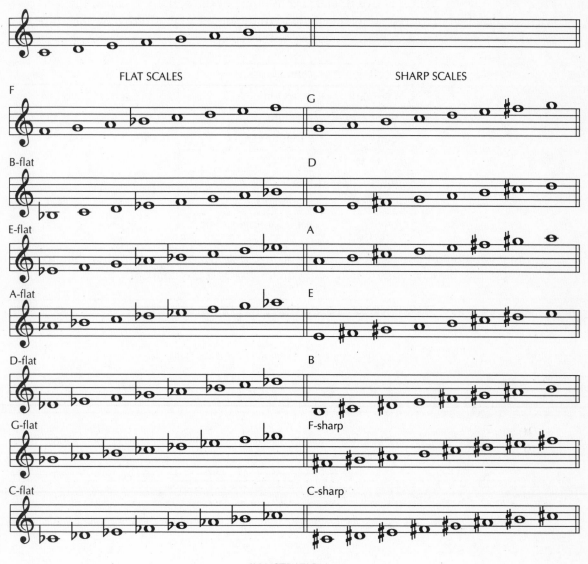

ILLUSTRATION 4

By tradition, the various steps of the scale, regardless of its key, have certain descriptive names. The first scale step, *do*, or the home tone, is called the *tonic*. The second tone of the scale, *re*, is called the *supertonic*, meaning "above the tonic." The third tone, *mi*, is called the *mediant* because it is the middle tone of the chord based on the tonic. (We will get to chords in a later chapter.) The fourth tone, *fa*, is called the *subdominant*, the "dominant below," since it is as far below the tonic as the *dominant* is above it. (This unlikely-sounding reasoning has been used for enough centuries that one can hardly hope to alter it at this late date.) The fifth tone, *sol*, is the *dominant*. It takes the highest position in the chord based on the tonic. This tone is dominant in many other respects as well, as we shall discover later on.

The sixth tone of the scale, *la*, is called the *submediant* because it is as far below the tonic as the mediant is above it. The seventh tone of the scale, *ti*, is called the *leading tone* because of its strong tendency to lead to the upper tonic. To review, these are the names for the various tones, or degrees, of the scale:

| | |
|---|---|
| Tone 1 (*do*) | tonic |
| Tone 2 (*re*) | supertonic |
| Tone 3 (*mi*) | mediant |
| Tone 4 (*fa*) | subdominant |
| Tone 5 (*sol*) | dominant |
| Tone 6 (*la*) | submediant |
| Tone 7 (*ti*) | leading tone |
| Tone 8 (*do*) | tonic, or upper tonic |

Keep in mind that these names refer to various steps in the scale rather than to specific pitches. Illustration 5 should help you understand this concept.

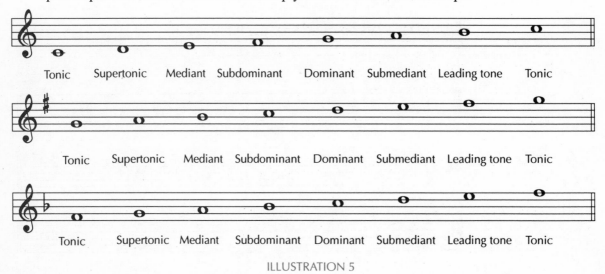

ILLUSTRATION 5

When you think you understand the above, do Exercise A on Worksheet #4 and have your teacher check your work.

## Key Signatures

When composers write music using specific scales, it would be possible, and correct, for them to write out the necessary flats or sharps for the changed scale notes each time the particular note appeared in the music. But this practice would make a lot of extra work for copyists, since in many scales the altered (flatted or sharped) notes appear quite frequently. The solution is for the composer to state at the beginning of the piece what flats or sharps are to be used throughout, and then leave it up to the performer to keep those notes in mind. We call this listing the *key signature.*

Let's go back for a moment to the scales mentioned in Illustration 4. We found that if we started on the note C, we could produce a major scale without using either flats or sharps. However, if we started on the note F, the scale wouldn't sound right unless we lowered the B to B-flat. And, if we started on G, we needed to raise F to F-sharp. The key signature for C major needs neither flats nor sharps; the key signature for F major calls for a B-flat; and the key signature for G needs an F-sharp. Play the three versions of the song, "America," found in Illustration 6. Notice how the B-flat in the second version and the F-sharp in the third version are necessary to make the melody sound correct. For comparison, play these versions using all natural notes in place of the flat or sharp. This is why the key of F has one flat (always B-flat), and the key of G has one sharp (always F-sharp). Furthermore, in all scales with more than one flat, the first flat to the left will be B-flat, and in all scales with more than one sharp, the first one to the left will be F-sharp.

ILLUSTRATION 6

Illustration 7 shows you the order in which the flats and sharps always appear, reading from left to right. At this point, we may remark on some curious facts. First, the order of the flats (B, E, A, D, G, C, F) is exactly the opposite of the order of the

ILLUSTRATION 7

sharps (F, C, G, D, A, E, B). Second, each successive flat occurs on a note five steps *below* the previous one (go five steps down from B to E; go five steps down from E to A; and so on), while each successive sharp occurs on a note five steps *above* the previous (go five steps up from F to C; go five steps up from C to G; and so on). When these flats and sharps are written on the staff, they are placed within the span of an octave so that they will all fit within a five-line staff; but the *order* in which they appear is determined by the up-or-down-five-steps rule. Spend some time learning exactly where on the staff the flats and sharps are placed, since you must put yours in the same places.

Illustration 7 shows all seven flats and sharps in the key signature. For signatures with less than seven flats or sharps, you need only start at the left and place the correct number of flats or sharps on the staff in the same order as in Illustration 7. For example, if the key signature has three flats, they will always be B, E, and A, in that order. Similarly, if the key signature has four sharps, they will always be F, C, G, and D, in that order.

You now know how to find the key signature for a major scale starting on any given note. But how can you tell the key of a piece from its key signature? There are three simple rules that apply.

1.  If there are no sharps or flats in the key signature, the key is C major.

2.  If there are sharps in the key signature, the sharp *farthest to the right* is the note *ti* (the leading tone) in the scale. To find *do*, simply name the note a half step above that sharp. For example, if there is only one sharp, F-sharp, that note is the leading tone in the scale. Go up one half step to the tonic; it is G, so the key signature is that of the key of G. This can be seen in Illustration 8A. In Illustration 8B, we have another example. The sharp farthest to the right is C-sharp; this becomes the leading tone, the tonic is therefore D, and the key is D.

ILLUSTRATIONS 8A and 8B

3.  If there are flats in the key signature, the flat farthest to the right is the note *fa* (the subdominant) in the scale. To find *do*, begin with *fa* as one, and count down to the fourth note. This note names the key. In Illustration 9A, the flat is B-flat; that note is the subdominant. Counting B-flat as one, count downward to the fourth note: B-flat, A, G, F. The key signature of one flat indicates the key of F major. In Illustration 9B, the flat farthest to the right is E-flat; that note is the

subdominant, and you count down to the tonic, which is B-flat (remember that B is already flat, according to the key signature). The key signature of two flats indicates the key of B-flat.

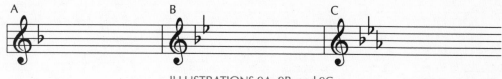

ILLUSTRATIONS 9A, 9B, and 9C

Now for a shortcut. In the key of B-flat, the *next-to-last* flat also names the key. This is true of any flat key with more than one flat. For instance, Illustration 9C shows a key signature with three flats. The last flat to the right (A-flat) is the subdominant; count down four to find the tonic. What key do you have? Now, simply **name** the next-to-last flat—in this case, E-flat. You should find that both systems give the same answer.

The following question sometimes arises: Are there any key signatures in which *both* flats and sharps appear? While such signatures are possible, they will never occur when the piece of music is in a major key. Play the scales in Illustration 10 and listen to the results. Be careful to observe the key signatures.

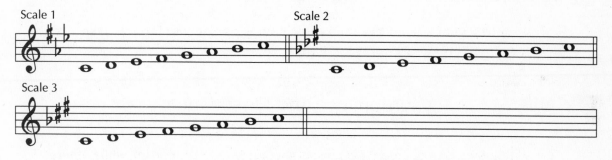

ILLUSTRATION 10

You may enjoy writing out songs you know using these scales. For example, in Illustration 11, "America" uses Scale 1, "Twinkle, Twinkle, Little Star" uses Scale 2, and "Red River Valley" uses Scale 3. Play them over for fun.

"America"

"Twinkle, Twinkle, Little Star"

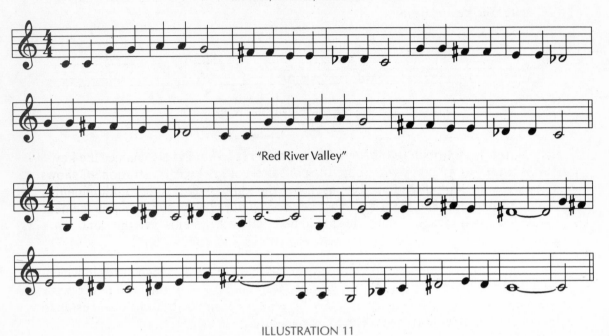

"Red River Valley"

ILLUSTRATION 11

When you think you understand key signatures, do Exercise B on Worksheet #4 and have your teacher check your work.

## Consonance and Dissonance

Within the major scale, certain tones sound more restful and final, while others sound restless and "incomplete" relative to the rest of the scale. To understand why this is, first play Illustration 2 over again (it's a C major scale). Then play Illustration 12. It doesn't sound complete, does it? One wants to hear the tonic, C, to complete the scale. It's a bit like reading a mystery whose last page is missing.

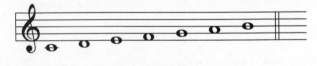

ILLUSTRATION 12

Tones that sound restful or complete are said to be *consonant*; tones that sound restless and unfinished are called *dissonant*. The tonic in any song is the most consonant tone, and most songs end on this tonic note. In Illustration 13 we see some common endings for songs. Notice that they both end on the tonic.

fa  mi  re  do    sol  la  ti  do

ILLUSTRATION 13

The tonic is obviously consonant; the supertonic is dissonant. It doesn't sound like a suitable ending note; instead it wants to move on to another one to finish. The supertonic can be *resolved*, or concluded, by moving either down to the tonic or up to the mediant, as in Illustration 14. The mediant is another consonant tone, though it's

re - mi    re - do

ILLUSTRATION 14

not as strongly consonant as the tonic. The subdominant is quite dissonant, and has a strong tendency to resolve down to the mediant, as in Illustration 15. The dominant is

do  ti  la  sol  fa - mi

ILLUSTRATION 15

another consonance, though less satisfactory as a final note than either the mediant or the tonic. The submediant is moderately dissonant, having a tendency to resolve to the dominant, as in Illustration 16. The leading tone is the most dissonant tone, and it

la - sol

ILLUSTRATION 16

almost always resolves up to the tonic, as in Illustration 17.

ti - do

ILLUSTRATION 17

These tendencies for tones of the scale generally hold true in any major scale in any key. The following table summarizes these tendencies for easy reference. As you examine melodies, or write them yourself, notice how often strong melodies move according to these tendencies.

| Scale tone | Description |
|---|---|
| tonic | consonant; final |
| supertonic | dissonant; moves a step up or down |
| mediant | consonant, but seldom the last note |
| subdominant | dissonant; moves down a half step |
| dominant | consonant, but less common as last note |
| submediant | dissonant; moves a step up or down |
| leading tone | dissonant; moves up a half step |

As technical studies, scales make good practice material for budding instrumentalists. They also make useful warm-up exercises for instrumentalists and vocalists. Scales are basic exercises for professional musicians because they rehearse the performer in the notes to be used in pieces of various keys. But, as melodies, scales seem to lack a certain something.

That "something" is variety. Scales are monotonously predictable, going up or down precisely an octave, or some multiple of an octave. One desires a bit more suspense, a feeling of unpredictability or drama, in a good melody. It is really a challenge to a performer to make a scale sound like something other than a mechanical exercise.

When you think you understand consonance and dissonance in the scale, do Exercise C on Worksheet #4 and have your teacher check your work.

## Exercise A

1. Using the necessary pattern of whole and half steps, write out the major scale that begins with the note given on each staff below. Remember to include flats and sharps as needed.

2. In each measure below, a note is given which represents the tonic. Beneath each measure is the name of a scale degree. Write the note that corresponds to that scale degree in the space to the right of the tonic. Remember to use flats and sharps. When you have finished, have your teacher check your work.

dominant     submediant     supertonic     subdominant     mediant     leading tone

## Exercise B

1. Write out the key signature for each of the scales as indicated below the measures.

E-flat     B     D     A-flat     E     D-flat     A     B-flat

2. On the blank below each measure, indicate the major key for the key signature.

## Exercise C

On the blank below each measure, identify the phrase ending as consonant or dissonant. Have your teacher check your work.

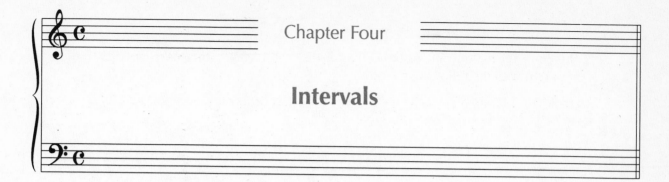

# Intervals

Diatonic scales make use of only whole and half steps; pentatonic scales make use of some steps that are larger than whole steps. Of course, there are many other possible distances between tones. The distance, in sound and in print, between any two tones is called an *interval*. We have already examined two types of interval, the half step and the whole step. Intervals take their names from the way they look when written down. From one written note to a note on the next line or space is called a *second* because if you count the lower note as one, the higher note would be step two. This can be seen in Illustration 1.

ILLUSTRATION 1

A diatonic scale, then, is a series of tones in which the adjacent written notes are a second apart. (We will get to the difference between a half-step second and a whole-step second shortly.)

Melodies, on the other hand, generally use many sizes of intervals. Let's examine two familiar melodies and see how they are made.

*"My Old Kentucky Home"*

Slowly

In this song, the melody moves basically stepwise, with a few rather narrow skips. Compare it with the following melody:

"Buffalo Gals"

Here, the motion is basically by skips, with only a few stepwise portions. We can see from these two examples that most melodies move both by steps and by skips, but that the proportion of each type of movement varies quite a bit from song to song.

Let's pause for a moment and think about what effects these two songs have on the listener. The first is slow, thoughtful, a bit sad, and homesick. The second is a lively dance tune, full of energy, almost boisterous. The stepwise movement of the first song and the skipwise movement of the second, combined with the different tempos, do much to reinforce the overall moods of the two songs. This is a trick worth remembering when you write your own music.

As we have said, stepwise intervals are called seconds. Other intervals are named in the same manner; that is, by calling the lower note "one" and counting up stepwise to the higher note. Illustration 2 shows the other intervals and their names. Of course,

ILLUSTRATION 2

all these intervals begin with C as the first note. Intervals of the same size (that is, intervals covering the same number of steps) have the same name, regardless of which two notes are involved. Study Illustration 3 to see how this works.

ILLUSTRATION 3

Now let's return to "My Old Kentucky Home." We can analyze the way the notes move in terms of the intervals used rather than in crude terms such as steps or skips. By the way, when two or more notes appear in succession on the same pitch, this is termed a *unison*, symbolized by a U. L means *lower*, and H means *higher*. These symbols are written below the notes in Illustration 4:

ILLUSTRATION 4

Compare this with "Buffalo Gals" in Illustration 5.

ILLUSTRATION 5

Now we're prepared to compare the melodic movement of these two songs, interval by interval. Notice that, while the total number of intervals in "My Old Kentucky Home" (38) is almost the same as the total in "Buffalo Gals" (39), the first song has many more higher or lower seconds (26) than the other (9). And "Buffalo Gals" has many more thirds (12) than "My Old Kentucky Home" (5). By making such comparisons among melodies, we can learn something of what makes different melodies sound smooth or lively. This is presented in Illustration 6.

|  | U | 2H | 2L | 3H | 3L | 5H | 5L | 6H |
|---|---|---|---|---|---|---|---|---|
| "My Old Kentucky Home" | 6 | 13 | 13 | 3 | 2 | 0 | 1 | 0 |
| "Buffalo Gals" | 16 | 2 | 7 | 5 | 7 | 1 | 0 | 1 |

ILLUSTRATION 6

# Major, Minor, and Perfect Intervals

So far, so good; but we need to refine our analysis still further. As you know, there are two different sizes of seconds, whole-step seconds and half-step seconds. How can we label them precisely? Whole-step seconds are called *major* seconds; half-step seconds are *minor* seconds. What makes them different is obviously the number of half steps (two or one) in each. On the keyboard, C to D is a major second because it has a black key between the two white keys. E to F, on the other hand, is a minor second since there is no black key between the white keys.

Some of the other intervals also come in major and minor forms. These may be thought of as combinations of major and minor seconds. For example, combining a major second (C to D) with a minor second (D to E-flat) produces a minor third (three half steps, from C to E-flat). This is only one example; *any* two notes a third apart, and whose distance is three half steps, make a minor third. Study the examples in Illustration 7, which are all minor thirds, although some of them do not use an accidental to make them minor.

minor thirds

ILLUSTRATION 7

Combining two major seconds results in a major third (four half steps: C to D and D to E make up the major third C to E). This, of course, suggests the possibility of combining two minor seconds to make a third. (We will discuss this special case later in the book.) Again, any third that has a combination of two adjacent major seconds makes a major third, as can be seen in Illustration 8.

major thirds

ILLUSTRATION 8

Unisons, fourths, fifths, and octaves do not come in major and minor versions; instead, in their basic forms, they are referred to as *perfect intervals*. A *perfect unison* (and there are imperfect ones) obviously contains no half steps. A perfect fourth combines two major seconds and one minor second (five half steps). A perfect fifth comprises three major seconds and one minor second (seven half steps). A *perfect octave* contains five major and two minor seconds, for a total of twelve half steps. Illustration 9 has examples of all these intervals.

Sixths and sevenths, like seconds and thirds, come in major and minor forms. A *minor sixth* comprises three major and two minor seconds (eight half steps). A *major*

ILLUSTRATION 9

*sixth* comprises four major seconds and one minor second (nine half steps). A *minor seventh* comprises four major seconds and two minor seconds (ten half steps), and a *major seventh*, five major seconds and one minor second (eleven half steps). Illustration 10 shows major and minor sixths and sevenths.

ILLUSTRATION 10

A word of caution about analyzing intervals. There are some intervals that can have two different names even though they have the same number of half steps between the notes. For example, in Illustration 11, you can see that there are ten half steps between the two notes. However, that does not make it a minor seventh. You should begin by working out what the *basic interval* is (third, fourth, fifth, or other) by calling the lower note "1" and counting up to the higher note. You can then see that in Illustration 11 we have a special kind of sixth rather than a minor seventh. We will return to this idea later in the book.

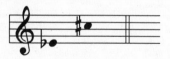

ILLUSTRATION 11

Now that you understand the principle, see if you can do Exercise A on Worksheet #5. Have your teacher check the answers.

There is a form of musical shorthand that is used to indicate the sizes of the various intervals. Major intervals are indicated by a capital *M* followed by a number (M2 for a major second, M3 for a major third, and so on). Minor intervals are symbolized by a lowercase *m* followed by a number (m6, m7). All perfect intervals are indicated by a capital *P* and a number (P1, P4, P5, P8).

The following chart summarizes the intervals and the number of half steps contained in each. Learn these intervals, both by construction and by sound. You will be using this information constantly from now on in this course.

| INTERVAL CONSTRUCTION | |
| --- | --- |
| **Interval** | **Number of half steps** |
| m2 | 1 |
| M2 | 2 |
| m3 | 3 |
| M3 | 4 |
| P4 | 5 |
| P5 | 7 |
| m6 | 8 |
| M6 | 9 |
| m7 | 10 |
| M7 | 11 |
| P8 | 12 |

Now, one last time, let's take a look at "My Old Kentucky Home," applying all the information above to an analysis. In Illustration 12 you see the intervals of the song indicated beneath the notes. Study this until you are certain that you understand every interval. Then work Exercise B on Worksheet #5.

ILLUSTRATION 12

# Harmonic Intervals

In our discussions so far, we have been talking about *melodic intervals*—intervals that occur when one tone follows another in a melody line. This, in fact, makes a pretty good working definition of a "melody": a succession of tones related to each other in terms of specific intervals. In this section, we shall focus on a different type of interval, the *harmonic interval*.

When two tones are sounded at the same time, the result is a harmonic interval. Each interval is identified in the same way as melodic intervals, that is, as a major third, a minor sixth, a perfect fifth, and so on. The only difference is that the two tones are sounded together, rather than in succession, and the result is called a harmonic, rather than a melodic, interval.

These harmonic intervals are the basic units from which all harmony is created, the bricks and mortar from which symphonies and cantatas are built. They are also basic material for everything else you will learn in the study of music theory. Obviously, then, harmonic intervals are of the greatest importance and must be thoroughly understood before you go any further.

The importance of harmony in music is, in some ways, like the importance of color in painting. Up to now, we have been working with successions of single tones—melodies, scales, and so on. This is rather like working with line in painting—one sketches with a pencil or draws with pen and ink. Line and shape are very important in painting, of course, but the use of color adds a new world of possibilities to the painter's vocabulary. So it is with harmony. Melody is necessary, but harmony adds a vast new dimension to music.

The analogy between color and harmony goes even further. Each color has its own distinctive character and emotional tone—exciting reds, cool greens, somber black. In a very similar way, each harmonic interval has a character and an emotional quality—clashing seconds, hollow fifths, placid sixths. Finally, just as colors can be mixed to produce new, subtle shades and effects, so harmonic intervals can be combined to produce a nearly endless variety of expressive sounds.

Some intervals seem to blend together so smoothly that you have difficulty telling whether one or two notes are sounding. The octave is the best example of this kind of interval. In other words, the harmonic octave is a very consonant interval. Other intervals are more or less consonant; some of them are quite dissonant. For example, a minor second is a very dissonant interval.

If you write out a scale containing all the twelve notes included within an octave, and then analyze the harmonic intervals between the first note (*do*) and each other note of the octave, you will note a curious fact: *The nearer to each end of the scale you get, the greater the dissonance of the interval.* Or, to turn the statement around, the greatest degrees of consonance, other than the unison and the octave, appear between the lowest note and those notes halfway between the notes of the octave. This is illustrated below. (The *very* middle interval, D to G-sharp in the following illustration, is a

ILLUSTRATION 13

special case that will be discussed later.) Play each of these intervals on a piano and listen to the degree of dissonance or consonance each produces.

Each harmonic interval in the octave has its own special sound, or flavor. With a little practice, you will be able to recognize the interval by its characteristic sound, without ever seeing the notes. Practice this type of recognition, for soon you will need this skill in well-developed form. Let's consider each interval's characteristic sound.

A *minor second* (*do* to lowered *re*, or *ti* to *do*) has so much "bite," such sharp dissonance, that it is seldom used by itself. It gives a feeling of great discord, of extreme restlessness or tension. When it is used, it is often on a weaker beat of the measure (such as beat two or beat four), or as a "passing" interval between a unison and a following consonance, as in Illustration 14. Whenever someone in band or

ILLUSTRATION 14

orchestra forgets to use a flat or sharp in the key signature, the result is a minor-second dissonance that stands out all too plainly.

A *major second* (*do* to *re*) is still dissonant, but not quite so edgy or discordant as the minor second. This is the interval used to harmonize the first six notes in the melody called "Chopsticks," as you can see from Illustration 15. The major second is a

ILLUSTRATION 15

tense and restless interval. Sometimes it is used for a moment of dense harmonic texture followed by a more consonant interval, as in Illustration 16.

ILLUSTRATION 16

A *minor third* (*do* to lowered *mi*) is reasonably consonant; it doesn't sound especially harsh or restless. It does not sound as final or solid as, say, a perfect fifth. A *major third* (*do* to *mi*) has a full, rich, consonant quality. It is quite stable, and usually has a cheerful, optimistic sound. When the notes of a scale are harmonized in thirds, both major and minor thirds appear, as in the interesting alternation shown in Illustration 17.

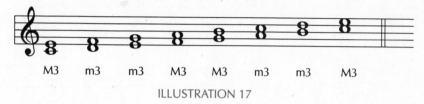

M3    m3    m3    M3    M3    m3    m3    M3

ILLUSTRATION 17

A *perfect fourth* (*do* to *fa*) is even more stable and consonant, but it is much less colorful and rich than the thirds. Although the interval itself is stable, it still has an air of dissonance, or incompleteness, about it when used because it is so often followed by a major third. Play and listen carefully to Illustration 18, and notice how the fourth "resolves" to a third.

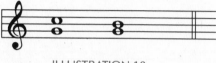

ILLUSTRATION 18

An *augmented fourth* (*do* to raised *fa*; the term *augmented* means "added to") is a very special interval with unique characteristics. This interval, which appears melodically in the major scale between the fourth and seventh steps (*fa* and *ti*; F and B, in C major), is sometimes called a tritone because it contains three whole steps (F to G, G to A, A to B). It has been condemned as "the devil in music" (*diabolus in musica*) since it is difficult to sing either melodically or harmonically. Oddly enough, this mid-scale interval is one of the more dissonant intervals because it provides no feeling of a home tone. Composers often use the tritone to help them move from one key to another in a composition. When the tritone is used harmonically in a composition, the two tones move by step in opposite directions, making a very satisfying ending, as in Illustration 19.

ILLUSTRATION 19

Next to the unison and the octave, the *perfect fifth* is the most consonant of the harmonic intervals. Although it is very stable, it has a colorless, "hollow" sound, with no feeling of either major or minor. Drones of a perfect fifth are often used to imitate bagpipe effects, as in Illustration 20. Perfect fifths are also used to represent Native American music, as in Illustration 21, or "Chinese" music, as in Illustration 22. In fact, neither Native American nor Chinese music uses perfect fifths as harmony except incidentally.

The sixths, like the thirds, are rich and colorful intervals without being dissonant. The *minor sixth* (*do* to lowered *la*) and the *major sixth* (*do* to *la*) sound similar, and

ILLUSTRATION 20

ILLUSTRATION 21

ILLUSTRATION 22

both occur in a scale harmonized in sixths, as in Illustration 23. In this instance, the scale occurs in the higher notes, each note harmonized a sixth below.

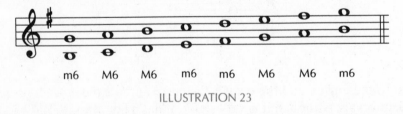

ILLUSTRATION 23

The *minor seventh* (*do* to lowered *ti*) is one of the most important dissonances in music because it appears in a special, very useful chord. The effect of the interval is restlessness and instability. A common harmonic progression involving the minor seventh occurs when the top tone of the interval drops a half step while the lower tone rises a perfect fourth, as in Illustration 24. The resultant major third is quite satisfying. The *major seventh* (*do* to *ti*) makes a very unstable, edgy dissonance. It usually appears when a harmonized melody "passes through" the seventh on its way to a

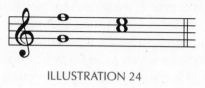

ILLUSTRATION 24

more consonant interval, as in Illustration 25. Composers and jazz arrangers often use

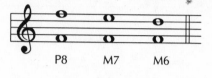

ILLUSTRATION 25

the major seventh by burying it in a dense chord. The other notes of the chord in which the seventh appears temper the dissonance and make it sound rich and full, rather than discordant, as in Illustration 26.

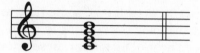

ILLUSTRATION 26

The following table summarizes the information we have discussed about harmonic intervals. Play each of these intervals, and listen carefully for its special characteristics until you can recognize each by ear when you hear it. These are the musical bricks from which all harmony is constructed, so it is most important that you be thoroughly familiar with them. In this table the key is C, and the letters describe the degree of consonance or dissonance.

| Interval | Name | Consonance | Interval | Name | Consonance |
|----------|------|------------|----------|------|------------|
| C to C | unison | VC | C to G | P5 | C |
| C to D-flat | m2 | VD | C to A-flat | m6 | C |
| C to D | M2 | D | C to A | M6 | C |
| C to E-flat | m3 | C | C to B-flat | m7 | D |
| C to E | M3 | C | C to B | M7 | VD |
| C to F | P4 | C | C to C | octave | VC |
| C to F-sharp | A4 | D | | | |

*Legend:* C=consonant; D=dissonant; V=very

Perhaps you have already noticed that the consonance descriptions of this table read exactly the same from the end to the beginning as from the beginning to the end. The reason for this fact becomes clear when we study these intervals in what is called inverted form. When you invert an interval, you simply take the bottom note of the interval and move it up an octave. If we do this to each interval in this table, we simply reverse the pattern of the notes in Illustration 13, and we have the pattern in Illustration 27. By comparing Illustration 13 with Illustration 27, we can see that when a second is inverted, it becomes a seventh, and when a third is inverted, it becomes a sixth. Similarly, an inverted fourth becomes a fifth, and so on. Going one step further,

ILLUSTRATION 27

an inverted *minor* second becomes a *major* seventh, and inverted *major* third becomes a *minor* sixth, but an inverted *perfect* fourth becomes a *perfect* fifth. This explains why seconds and sevenths or thirds and sixths have similar consonant qualities.

Major, minor, perfect, augmented—it's a lot to keep in mind, and we aren't at the end of it yet. For now, however, we will take some time to absorb what we have covered. Play the intervals over and over, trying to learn the quality of each so that you can identify it when you hear it. Listen for these intervals in the music you perform in school; look at music scores and see how much you can understand. In addition, do Exercise C on Worksheet #5 until you can identify all the intervals perfectly. Intervals are the letters of the alphabet for all music!

# WORSHEET #5

## Exercise A

Identify each of the following intervals as major (M), minor (m), or perfect (P), and as a second, third, fourth, and so on.

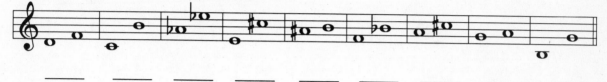

## Exercise B

In the space below the notes of this song, "Buffalo Gals," identify the interval between each pair of notes, and the direction in which it moves (using *U*, *H*, and *L*, for unison, higher, and lower, respectively).

## Exercise C

In the space below each of these measures, identify the interval between the two notes. Use *P* for perfect, *M* for major, *m* for minor, *A* for augmented, and *d* for diminished.

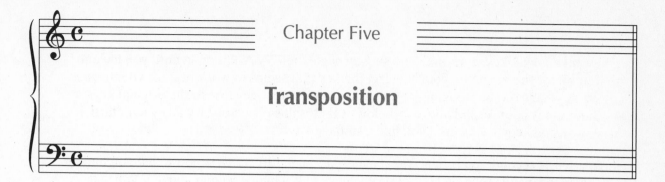

# Chapter Five

# Transposition

If you have ever played or sung a song that was too high or too low, or just in a "bad" key for your instrument, you may have wished that there were some way to rewrite the piece in a better key or range. In this chapter, you will learn to do just that.

Let's begin with a familiar song. Illustration 1 shows the first half of "Yankee Doodle," written in the key of F major. Assume that, for some reason, this is not a

ILLUSTRATION 1

convenient key for your purposes. The following steps will allow you to change the key of that song, a process known as *transposition*.

## Method for Transposition

The first step is to select a better key. Let's suppose the reason you want to change the key is to bring the song more comfortably into your voice range. If the song is too high as written, you'll want to pick a key slightly lower—E, perhaps, or E-flat. If, on the other hand, you have a good high register and don't sound as full on the lower notes, you may want to raise the key to G, or even A.

Begin by singing the song with different starting pitches. If the original song is too high for comfort, play an E on the piano and, beginning on that pitch, *sing the whole song through*. If it is still too high, then start on E-flat. Continue this process until you find a starting note that allows you to sing the whole song comfortably. If you want a *higher* key, start on G and sing through; then try A-flat or A, until you have to strain for the top notes. Finally, select the key that seems to work best for you. In any case, when you start looking for a new key, begin with one close to the original key—a minor or major second above or below. If that isn't satisfactory, try a key a bit farther away, and keep trying until you find a suitable key.

The second step is to arrive at a new key signature. Let's suppose that you find that starting the song on G works well. Since G is a major second above F, you will need a key signature for the key, which is a major second above F; this key is G (one sharp), as you can see in Illustration 2.

ILLUSTRATION 2

The third step is to go through the entire song, note by note, writing each note a major second higher than the original note. This is Exercise A on Worksheet #6; when you have finished, play the song over and see if it sounds correct to you. Then check the answer key at the end of Worksheet #6 for the correct transposition.

For our second practice with transposition, we will use "America, the Beautiful," written in the key of C, as seen in Illustration 3. Notice that while the original key is C,

ILLUSTRATION 3

the song starts on the note G, which is *sol* in the key of C. Follow the procedure, as outlined above, of singing the song through and starting on different notes until you find one that puts you in a comfortable range. Let's suppose that you find starting on F works best. Since this note is one step lower than G, you will need a key that is also one step lower, which is the key of B-flat. The song will still start on *sol*, of course, and

F is *sol* in the key of B-flat (two flats). The song must be written out a whole step *below* the original key.

It is important here to keep in mind that we are concerned with the *key* of the original version, not just the *starting note*. Your first assignment, "Yankee Doodle," was in the key of F and started on F, which is *do* in that key. "America, the Beautiful," which is in the key of C, actually begins on G, or *sol* in that key. Therefore, when you transpose this song, you must begin on *sol* in the new key, rather than *do*.

You are now ready to do Exercise B on Worksheet #6, which is to transpose "America, the Beautiful" into the key of B-flat. Here are a few checkpoints to keep you on track: The first note of measure 3 in your transposition will be an E-flat; since you have written this flat in the key signature at the beginning, you do not need to mark it as an accidental. The C-sharp in measure 7, however, does present a special problem. Remember that in the original (C) version, what is wanted is a note one half step higher than *do* in the key. When transposed to B-flat, however, the note one half step higher than *do* will be B-natural, not B-sharp. You can see that a sharp in the original version will not necessarily turn out to be a sharp in the transposed version; similarly, a flat in the original may become a natural in the transposition. Later in the chapter, we will discuss transcribing accidentals at length.

After you have completed the transposition, play it over on the piano. If it sounds right, have your teacher check your version carefully, note by note, against the model.

Now let's suppose that when you sang "America, the Beautiful," you decided that the key was too *low*. In Exercise C on the worksheet, transpose the song into the key of D, one whole step *higher* than the original key. Remember that there will be two sharps in the key signature, and that the first note will be an A. In this transposition, the first note of the seventh measure will be D-sharp (a half step above D). When you have completed the transposition, play it and check it by ear; then have your teacher check it note by note.

## B-flat Transposition

In Illustration 4, you see a well-known hymn, "God of Our Fathers," written in the key of E-flat. If you play this melody on the piano and have a trumpet or clarinet player play the music with you, it will immediately be apparent that something is drastically wrong; the piano and the wind instrument are a major second apart on each note. The reason for this is that the trumpet and the clarinet (and certain other instruments) are what we term "transposing" instruments. This means that their music must be transposed from the original (or concert) pitch in order to fit with non-transposing instruments, such as the piano. You may notice that music for trumpet or clarinet is marked, "B-flat trumpet (or clarinet)." This means that when one of these instruments plays its written C, the pitch that is actually heard is a piano's B-flat. In order to sound

"God of Our Fathers"

ILLUSTRATION 4

right with such concert-pitch instruments as the piano, flute, or violin, the music must be transposed up a whole step.

The first step in transposing "God of Our Fathers" for trumpet or clarinet, then, is to select a key a whole step above the original. A whole step above E-flat is F, so you will put the key signature for F (one flat) at the beginning of the transposed line. Since the song begins on *do*, which is E-flat in the original key, you will start with *do*, or F, in the transposed line. (To help you find the proper key signatures, a special table at the end of this book lists all the keys and their signatures.) You should now work Exercise D on Worksheet #6. Think carefully about how you will treat the accidentals when you make the transcription. As always, play your transposition over and have your teacher check it.

The trumpet and clarinet play pitches that are only a whole step lower than the written pitch. Other instruments also use a B-flat transposition, but the sounding note is a major ninth (an octave and a major second) below the written pitch. Two of these are the bass clarinet and the tenor saxophone. If a baritone part is written in treble clef, it also sounds a major ninth below the written pitch. When you write for these instruments, you must remember to take the extra octave into account. This is summarized in Appendix B.

## E-flat Transposition

When a B-flat transposing instrument plays a written C, the pitch that sounds is B-flat. Similarly, when an E-flat transposing instrument such as the alto saxophone or the alto clarinet plays a written C, the pitch produced is an E-flat. In both the alto clarinet and the alto saxophone, the pitch is a major sixth *below* the written pitch. If the alto saxophone were to play the written notation in Illustration 5A, the pitches actually produced would be those in Illustration 5B. Study these carefully to be sure you understand the principle involved.

If you are transcribing a concert-pitch part, such as a vocal part with piano accompaniment, for solo alto saxophone, you must take each note and transpose it *up*

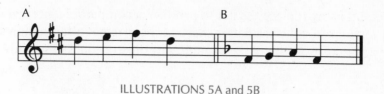

ILLUSTRATIONS 5A and 5B

a major sixth, reversing the process described above. In each of these instances, remember that the instrument will be sounding a sixth *below* the written pitch.

Occasionally a band will include an E-flat clarinet for playing the very high parts. Unlike the alto saxophone or alto clarinet, this instrument plays pitches a minor third *above* the written note. The E-flat baritone saxophone plays pitches an octave and a major sixth (a major thirteenth) below the written pitch.

You are now ready for Exercise E on Worksheet #6. Write the melody of "Ach, Du Lieber! Augustin" for alto saxophone. Remember that the notes for the instrument must be *higher* than the concert-pitch notes. Play the result over and listen for errors; have your teacher check it.

## Transposing Accidentals

As in the case of B-flat transposition, accidentals need special consideration. Suppose we are transposing Illustration 6 from piano to alto clarinet. The alto clarinet

ILLUSTRATION 6

part will be written in the key of G, and this excerpt will begin on F-sharp. The second note will be G. How shall we write the third note? You simply do the same thing in the new key; one half step above G would be G-sharp. (It could be A-flat, but then you would simply have to cancel the flat for the fourth note.) As you can see, a natural in the concert key may become a sharp in the transposed version.

The same logic applies to lowering tones. If a piano part has the notes in Illustration 7, the transposed part for alto clarinet (in G) would have the notes A, G, F-natu-

concert                                    transposed

ILLUSTRATION 7

ral, E. The natural may replace the flat to produce a comparable interval in the transposed version. Of course, a flat or sharp in the original often remains a flat or sharp in the transposition. Study the examples in Illustration 8 to see how this might happen.

ILLUSTRATION 8

Now test your understanding of the above by doing Exercise F on the worksheet.

## F Transposition

When you write music for band or orchestra, you need to master at least one more common transposition, and that is the one for instruments in F (the French horn and the English horn). When either of these instruments plays a written C, the instrument sounds the F below that C, as in Illustration 9. Therefore, it is necessary to transpose the part *upwards* a perfect fifth. Since the transposition is up such a large

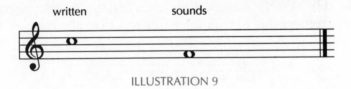

ILLUSTRATION 9

interval, notes *written* on the lower treble staff actually *sound* on the upper bass staff, as in Illustration 10. This fact must be kept in mind constantly when you are writing parts for these instruments.

ILLUSTRATION 10

## Other Transpositions

The above transpositions—B-flat, E-flat, and F—are the most common ones used in instrumental music, especially for band instruments. However, there are a few other transpositions that you may find occasionally. In band music of the early 1900's, one often finds a part for D-flat piccolo. To transpose a part for this instrument, you can use the same rule as above; that is, find a pitch a half step below the written key and apply the signature for that key.

Orchestral music occasionally calls for a clarinet in A. This means, of course, that when the instrument plays a written C, the actual pitch is A; the written C scale is actually the scale of A (three sharps). To transpose for this instrument, you must use a key signature for a key three half steps higher than the written key.

## Final Project

To summarize what you have learned in this chapter, we'll use the short chorale for three voices—soprano, alto, and bass—found in Illustration 11. First we'll arrange this chorale for three woodwind instruments: flute, B-flat clarinet, and E-flat alto saxophone.

ILLUSTRATION 11

Begin by working out the key signatures for the various instruments. The flute needs no change of key signature, since it is a non-transposing instrument. The clarinet part should be written a whole step higher, putting it in the key of C major. The alto saxophone part will be written a major sixth higher, in the key of G major.

Next, it is necessary to arrive at the starting pitch for each instrument. Again, the flute, which will play the melody, will simply play the top notes in our original score, starting with the D (*mi* in the key of B-flat). The clarinet, which will play the alto part, begins on *sol* (F) in the original score; therefore, it must begin on *sol* in its transposed key, the note one step higher (G). Finally, the first note in the bass part of the original is *do* (B-flat), so the alto saxophone will play *do* in its transposed key, which is the G that is a major sixth above bass clef B-flat. Notice that the clarinet and the alto saxophone both play the same written note, but that they sound pitches a fifth apart.

From this point on, the parts can be written out by placing each note the proper interval above or below the previous note, exactly as the parts appear in the original score. You should now complete Exercise G on Worksheet #6. You will see that the first note of each part is given, along with the key signatures. Once you have completed your transcription, play the result with the indicated instruments. If you've made an error, you'll hear it! Now end the work in this chapter by completing Exercise H on the worksheet. First transpose the concert key of the whole piece to F. Then arrange the chorale for B-flat trumpet, French horn in F, and baritone horn (bass clef) in C. Play the result and check your accuracy.

## Table of Keys and Key Signatures

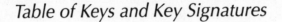

# Table of Written Notes and Their Sounding Pitches

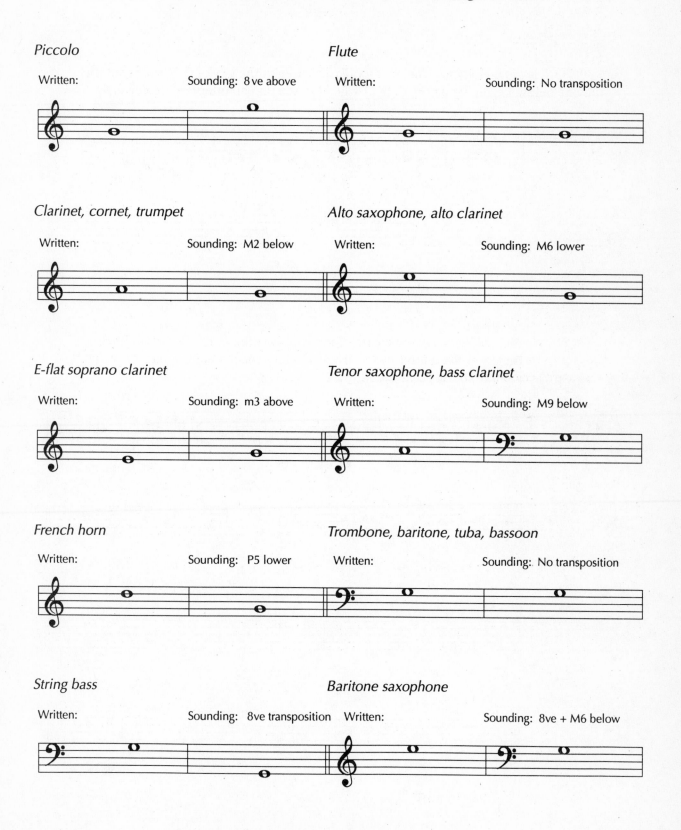

## Exercise A

Here is the melody to "Yankee Doodle," written in the key of C. Write it out on the line below, beginning on the note G. Check to see that all intervals are correct.

## Exercise B

Here is the melody to "America, the Beautiful," written in the key of C. Transpose it to the key of B-flat on the staves below. Double-check the intervals for which there are accidentals in the original.

## Exercise C

On the staves below, write out the melody to "America, the Beautiful" in the key of D.

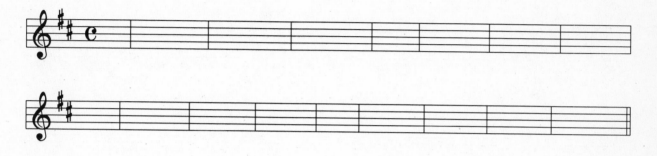

## Exercise D

Here is the melody to "God of Our Fathers," written in the key of C. Transpose it to the key of F, writing out the notes below the original.

## Exercise E

Here is the melody to "Ach, Du Lieber! Augustin." Transpose it for alto saxophone.

## Exercise F

Here is the melody to "The Navy Hymn." Transpose it for B-flat clarinet.

## Exercise G

Arrange the following chorale for flute, clarinet, and alto saxophone, making the necessary transpositions for the parts. The first note of each part is given, as is the key signature of the transposed part. The flute part can be taken exactly from the model.

## Exercise H

Arrange the same chorale for trumpet, French horn, and baritone (bass clef) in the key of F concert. Write the transposed key signatures for the various instruments.

Trumpet

French horn

Baritone, bass clef

ANSWER KEY

## Chapter Six

# Harmonizing a Melody

Whenever you sing or play a song, you are probably most aware of the melody; aside from the words, melody is what most songs are "about." However, you very rarely perform a melody by itself, without any accompanying parts. These accompanying parts enrich and decorate the melody such that it sounds quite bland and colorless without them. The accompaniment is usually the harmony part, which the composer or arranger has worked out to fit with that melody.

## Parallel Harmony

Musical harmony has been around for quite some time—over one thousand years in European music, the music on which ours is based. Naturally, over all that time, the writing of harmony has developed into a complex art, with many principles established for writing effective harmonizations. Sometimes, for some melodies, the technique of *parallel harmony* is very effective. As the name suggests, parallel harmonization uses one harmonic interval—typically a third or a sixth—for all notes of the melody. Illustration 1 shows a melody written by French composer Jacques Offenbach, called "Barcarolle."

ILLUSTRATION 1

It can easily be harmonized by writing notes a third above the notes in the melody. Play Illustration 2 on the piano and notice the effect of *parallel thirds.*

ILLUSTRATION 2

This makes a smooth, effective harmonization of Offenbach's melody. The only problem is that the melody, being the lower line of notes, is made rather ambiguous by the harmony part, since one always tends to hear the highest notes as the melody. Which is the melody, we wonder, the higher or the lower notes? We can clarify this piece by inverting the harmony line downward an octave. Now we have a melody (the top notes) harmonized by *parallel sixths* below, as in Illustration 3.

ILLUSTRATION 3

This simple technique of parallel harmony produces reasonably good harmonizations for a surprising number of songs. In Illustration 4, for example, the song "Amer-

ILLUSTRATION 4

ica" is harmonized in parallel sixths. There are a few spots that may not sound quite right, but on the whole, this is a successful harmonization.

The melody of "Twinkle, Twinkle, Little Star" is given in Illustration 5. Harmonize it in parallel sixths below, and then play the result. Does it make a satisfactory harmonization?

ILLUSTRATION 5

Some songs are harmonized better by using thirds *below* the melody, rather than above it. The beginning of a song called "Whispering Hope" is given in Illustration 6. Notice that it is harmonized in parallel thirds below the melody, except for the last two notes. Try harmonizing these two notes in thirds below, and then compare that with the written ending.

ILLUSTRATION 6

As a rule, melodies that begin with the *sol* or *mi* of their key should be harmonized in thirds below; melodies that begin on *do* should be harmonized by a third above or a sixth below. It may improve the harmonization of a third below to make the last note a unison, as in the version of "London Bridge" found in Illustration 7.

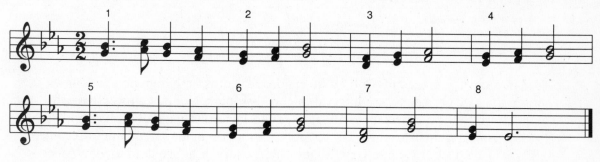

ILLUSTRATION 7

Intervals other than thirds or sixths may be used for parallel harmonizations, but the results usually sound quite strange. Many centuries ago, in the music of the Roman Catholic church, melodies were harmonized in parallel fourths or fifths, as in Illustration 8. The result is a hollow-sounding harmony entirely unlike the thirds-and-

ILLUSTRATION 8

sixths richness you are probably used to. It is now used as a special effect, but it is not one that can be used often. Notice what happens to Offenbach's tune when it is harmonized in fourths, as in Illustration 9. Compare the sound of this harmonization with the version in Illustration 3.

ILLUSTRATION 9

Parallel fifths sound as hollow as fourths, since fifths and fourths are simply inversions of each other. In Illustration 10, the melody of a well-known song is harmonized in parallel fifths above.

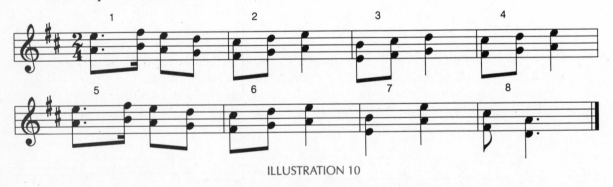

ILLUSTRATION 10

Harmonizing in seconds or their inversions, sevenths, is seldom done in our culture, since we consider these intervals highly dissonant. Not all cultures agree; in southeastern Europe, especially in Bulgaria, Yugoslavia, and parts of Greece and Romania, singers and instrumentalists happily harmonize in major and minor seconds, and even in quarter or three-quarter tones. These intervals are seldom used in American music. Hungarian composer Béla Bartók wrote a set of books of piano studies entitled *Mikrokosmos*. Book II of the set has several interesting sections. Number 63, subtitled "Buzzing," is harmonized entirely in seconds and sevenths. Number 62 is entitled "Minor Sixths in Parallel Motion," while number 56 is "Melody in Tenths," a tenth being an octave plus a third. If you can obtain a copy, play these easy pieces and notice the effects Bartók achieves.

Sometimes harmonies in seconds or sevenths are used for comic effect. In Illustrations 11A and B, "Yankee Doodle" is harmonized, first in sevenths, then in seconds. Try them and see how they sound.

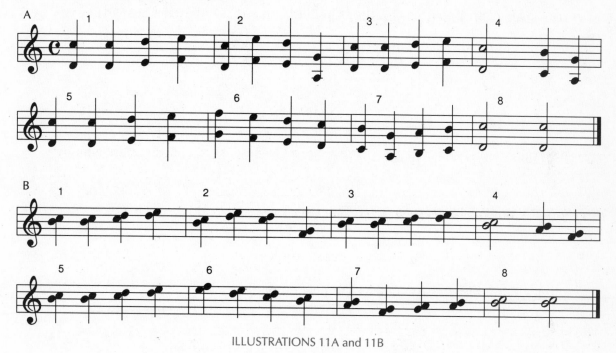

ILLUSTRATIONS 11A and 11B

To summarize parallel harmonizations: They are useful for some melodies, but are rather restricted in use since many pieces do not harmonize well in parallel motion. Thirds and sixths are most common and most effective; fourths and fifths are hollow sounding and are normally used only for special effects; and seconds and sevenths are dissonant, and sometimes used for comical effects.

Test your understanding of parallel harmonization by completing Exercise A on Worksheet #7.

## Chord Construction

Parallel harmonizations normally involve the sounding of two notes at one time. It is possible, however, to have more than two notes sound together—three, four, five, or even more are used quite frequently. When three or more tones sound together, the result is called a *chord*. Chords can be made up of *any* three or more tones. Some chords are made up of seconds; these are often called *tone clusters* because the notes are grouped tightly together like a cluster of grapes, as in Illustration 12. Chords may

ILLUSTRATION 12

also be made up of fourths or fifths, as in Illustration 13: Or they can be made up of

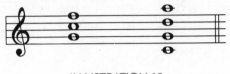

ILLUSTRATION 13

intervals of no standard size, as in Illustration 14. Most chords, however, are built by

ILLUSTRATION 14

placing thirds one above another, as in Illustration 15.

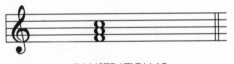

ILLUSTRATION 15

This basic, three-tone, third-on-third chord is called a *triad*. Triads are constructed by writing a note (F, for example), adding a second note a third above it (FA), and then adding still another third above the second note (FAC). The result is called a triad in *root position*. The triad takes its name from the bottom (or root) note in its root position, in this case, F. We would call this triad the "F triad" or the "F chord." At this point, you should complete Exercise B on Worksheet #7 and have your teacher check your work.

Like intervals, chords also come in major and minor forms. A *major chord* has a major third on the bottom of the triad and a minor third on top. For example, the C major chord has a major third from C to E (two whole steps) on the bottom of the triad, and a minor third from E to G (one and one half steps) on the top, as may be seen in Illustration 16A. Similarly, the F major chord has a major third from F to A on the bottom, and a minor third from A to C on the top (Illustration 16B).

ILLUSTRATIONS 16A and 16B

*Minor chords* have the opposite arrangement; that is, a minor third on the bottom and a major third on the top. For example, the A minor chord has a minor third from A to C on the bottom, and a major third from C to E on the top, as in Illustration 17A. Similarly, the D minor chord has a minor third from D to F on the bottom, and a major third from F to A on top (Illustration 17B).

ILLUSTRATIONS 17A and 17B

Chords can be built on any note by the same process of beginning with a note and adding notes at a major or minor third above the lower note. Chords are usually made based on the notes of a major or minor scale. When chords are based on the notes of the scale, the notes above the root are taken from the appropriate notes of that scale. When we make a C chord in the scale of C major, for example, we spell it CEG, and not CE-flatG or CEG-sharp, because those other notes do not occur in the C-major scale. This bring us to what might be called the *grammar* of chords.

The term *grammar* usually refers to the way in which words in a sentence relate to one another. Words used in isolation convey very little meaning to the listener: "happily" or "dinosaur" or "running" all transmit images, but there is no ongoing flow of action until words are arranged in such a manner as to sketch a story line. The simplest type of sentence is the familiar subject-verb-object sequence, as in "Loretta writes music." Here we have a subject or proposition (Loretta), a word suggesting action or motion (writes), and a satisfying conclusion of the word sequence (music). From this point onward, grammar consists mainly of embellishments on this basic sentence.

In a similar way, individual chords may be interesting or set a mood by themselves, but there is no sense of musical action, development, or flow until a sequence of chords is played. Furthermore, each chord of a scale relates to all the others so that some are passive (like subjects and objects) while some are active (like verbs), and some are more or less active than others. Finally, more complex chord sequences may be made by simply elaborating on these basic chord progressions.

Each chord of the scale has a special character in relation to all the other chords of the same scale. These chords are identified by the number of the root note in the scale. However, Roman numerals are used to identify chords, whereas Arabic numerals identify individual notes, as may be seen in Illustration 18.

ILLUSTRATION 18

In a major key, the I chord is always major, and it is the most consonant chord of all. The I chord is almost invariably the final chord in a piece of music, since it establishes *do* in the key. To end on any other chord would sound incomplete, if not bizarre. The II chord in a major key is always minor, and therefore is never used as a consonance, since it lacks the major quality of the basic scale. The II chord must be followed by some other chord.

The III chord is also minor, and thus also dissonant. It also must be followed by some other chord. The IV and V chords are both major. They play a most important role in chord progressions, as we shall see later. Even though they are major, they hardly ever serve as ending chords. Since they are both so far from the sound of the I chord, ending on either of these chords would give the effect of changing the basic key.

The VI chord is another minor chord, and ordinarily it is followed by other chords. The VII chord is a very special type of triad. If you study it carefully, you will notice that the lower third is minor, suggesting a minor chord. However, the upper third is also minor; this combination of minor third on minor third gives us a new chord form, a *diminished* chord. This type of chord is quite dissonant, and it has no character or feeling of being "in" any particular scale or key. This characteristic makes the chord, from one point of view, a weak one; yet it also makes the chord especially valuable for other purposes, such as changing key, as we shall see later. In writing music, a good composer or arranger takes advantage of the qualities each chord possesses.

In Illustration 19, you can see the chords of the major scale. The I, IV, and V

ILLUSTRATION 19

chords are always major; the II, III, and VI chords are minor; and the VII is a diminished chord. Once you have studied all of this, complete Exercise C on the worksheet and have your teacher check it.

# Chords in Minor Keys

We have been discussing major scales and keys until now; however, there are other possible scales, and even keys. The most common are the minor scales and their companion keys. The sound of music in minor keys is quite different from that of major keys. Where major-key music is often happy, triumphant, or serene in mood, minor-key music is often sad, ominous, or turbulent-sounding. "We Are Climbing Jacob's Ladder," "Twinkle, Twinkle, Little Star," and "Yankee Doodle" are all songs in major keys; "Let My People Go," "Joshua Fit the Battle of Jericho," and "When Johnny Comes Marching Home Again" are all songs in minor keys.

The technical difference between major and minor scales lies in their intervals. The pattern for the minor scale is found in the white key notes from A to A:

| A | | B | | C | | D | | E | | F | | G | | A |
|---|---|---|---|---|---|---|---|---|---|---|---|---|---|---|
| | w | | h | | w | | w | | h | | w | | w | |

Compare this with the intervals of the C major scale. Notice that the differences are mainly in the intervals from the second to the third notes, the fifth to the sixth notes, and the seventh to the eighth notes.

We term this scale the *A minor scale*, and it has a key signature of no sharps or flats. By using the same intervals, you can start minor scales on any note, just as you can major scales. Sine A minor has the same key signature as C major, we call it the *relative minor* scale of C major; although they start on different notes, they have the same key signature. The C major scale is the *relative major* scale of A minor. The relative minor of a major scale always begins on the sixth note (*la*) of the major scale; the relative major of a minor scale always begins on the third note of the minor scale. This is true no matter what the key signature may be.

Chords based on the minor scale naturally follow a different pattern. This pattern corresponds to the chords based on the relative minor scale, that is from *la* to *la* of the major scale. The i chord of a minor key is a minor chord (it is the same chord as the VI chord of the relative major), and it serves as the "home" chord of the piece. The ii chord in minor is diminished; the III in minor is a major chord. Since its sound suggests a change in mode from minor to major, it is not frequently used. The iv in minor is a minor chord, and one of the most important.

The v chord in minor is minor in its natural form, but it is usually made major by raising the third of the chord a half step, with the use of an accidental. (This is made necessary when chords are written in a chord progression; we will return to this in a later section.) In minor, VI is a major chord, as is VII. Like the III chord, these chords contradict the minor feeling of the key, and so are seldom used. Illustration 20 shows the chords of the minor scale: i and iv are minor; ii is diminished; III, VI, and VII are major; and V is altered to make it major.

I    II    III    IV    V    VI    VII    I

ILLUSTRATION 20

## Writing Chord Numbers

There are some generally accepted conventions regarding writing chord numbers, and which we will use in this book. Each major chord is symbolized by a Roman numeral written in uppercase (or capital) letters: I, IV, V (in major). Minor chords are written in lowercase (or small) letters: ii, iii, vi (in major). To distinguish easily between them when writing a manuscript, use heavy bars across the tops and bottoms of uppercase letters, but use *no* crossbars either above or below lowercase letters: I ii iii IV V vi. The diminished chord is written in lowercase form, followed by a superscript o: vii°. In this way, the reader can see at a glance whether the chord is major, minor, or diminished: I ii iii IV V vi vii°.

The chords of a minor scale will be represented by different chord symbols than the major: i ii° III iv V VI VII. Again, at a glance, one can tell whether the piece is major or minor by examining the pattern of the chords. Remember that the major V chord appears because the chord is altered; in its natural form, it would be minor (v). Test your understanding of this section by completing Exercise D on Worksheet #7.

## Block Chording

If you have ever played a guitar, ukulele, or autoharp, you know that chords are usually used as the background for melodies. Perhaps you have seen songs with symbols for chords written above (or below) the melody, as in Illustration 21. Remember that the letter indicating the chord specifies the root of that chord. Capital letters indicate that a major chord is to be used. If you were to write out the song in Illustration 21 with the indicated chords, it would look like Illustration 22. The Roman numerals for those chords in the key have been included. Try Illustration 22 on the piano and see how it sounds.

Thus far, we have used major chords. In Illustration 23, we have a minor-key song that uses both major and minor chords; notice the Roman numerals representing the chords. Minor chords are often symbolized by a capital letter indicating the root, followed by a lowercase *m*. Examples would be Gm, Dm, B-flat m, F-sharp m. You will also find these symbols in Illustrations 23A and 23B. When we write out the chords for this song, as in Illustration 23B, we must remember to use an A major V

"Skip to My Lou"

ILLUSTRATION 21

ILLUSTRATION 22

chord (AC-sharpE). Since there is no C-sharp in the key signature, it must be written in as an accidental each time the chord appears (except, of course, when that note, C, is repeated in the same measure). Test your understanding of this by completing Exercise E on the worksheet.

Now let's run the process backward. In Illustration 24 is a harmonized version of a song called "Vesper Hymn." Decide which chords are used; on a separate sheet of paper, write the letter names of the chords and give them their Roman numeral designations. Check the answers with your teacher.

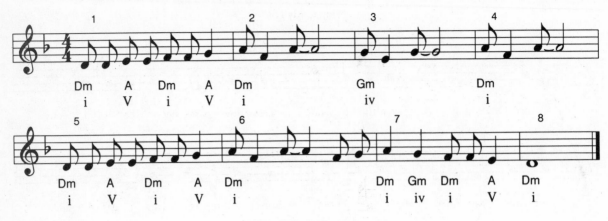

ILLUSTRATION 23A

ILLUSTRATION 23B

ILLUSTRATION 24

# Harmonizing a Song with No Given Chords

By now you should be quite comfortable with the names of chords and their numbers. Suppose, however, that you have a melody with *no* indicated chords. How does one decide which chords to use? For our exercise, we will use the American folk song "On Top of Old Smoky," found in Illustration 25.

ILLUSTRATION 25

To begin with, you should keep in mind that the home tone (*do*) and the home chord (I) are the most important in the key. Songs almost invariably end on the I chord; if they don't, they sound like they are in a different key. Songs often begin with the I chord as well, since that chord immediately establishes the key's sound to the listener's ear. So you should begin by discovering if the I chord will fit the melody at the beginning.

The first principle when doing your own harmonizations is to use as few chords as are absolutely necessary per measure in the basic harmonization. If you want to add other chords later, you can always add them, once the basic harmonization is worked out.

The second principle is to stay with the same chord until it no longer fits the melody well. When it doesn't fit, try other basic chords (I, IV, V or the minor chords) until you find one that sounds exactly right.

Examine the first four notes of the melody—C, C, E, G. Each of these notes is found in the I chord in the key of C, so obviously that chord will fit these notes. So far, so good.

The next measure requires a bit more thought. Chord changes are usually made on a strong beat of a measure, such as beat 1 in $\frac{3}{4}$ time, or beats 1 and 3 in $\frac{4}{4}$ time. Since our song is in 3, the chord change should come at the beginning of the measure, and that chord should be held throughout the measure, if possible.

At first glance, it might appear logical to harmonize the C in the second full measure with the C chord. After all, the previous measure was harmonized with I, so shouldn't it just carry over to the second measure? The problem with this reasoning is that the second note in this measure, A, is *not* part of the C chord. We need a chord that contains *both* the A and the C.

In the key of C, there are two chords that contain both of these notes, the F chord (IV) and the Am (vi). Illustrations 26A and 26B show these two chords in the second full measure. Play them both over and listen to how they sound. Decide which one you prefer.

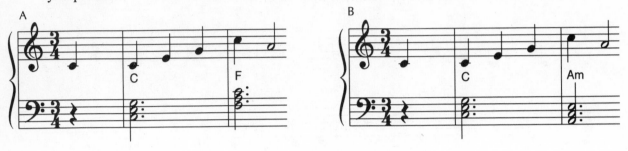

ILLUSTRATIONS 26A and 26B

Most people will probably prefer the F chord to the A minor for this harmonization. However, it is extremely important that you feel free to try out different, sometimes unusual, solutions to problems in music. *Music is not mathematics; there is no one right answer to a problem, with all others being wrong.* There are "better" and "worse" solutions, and the F chord is probably better in this situation. But a clever arranger or composer will often make a trite song sound fresh and interesting by using the "wrong" chord effectively in the harmonization.

Look ahead to the third full measure and you will see another reason why the F chord in measure 2 is a better solution. The last note of the measure is F. If we had used an A minor chord in measure 2, we would now have to change the chord in measure 3, since F is not a note in the A minor chord. This agrees with the second principle, to stay with a given chord until you need to change.

In measure 4, we have a scalewise melody, and it is obvious that no chord we have mentioned has F, G, and A in it. We could harmonize each note, but another way to treat the measure is to call the G a *passing tone*, a stepping stone between the F and the A. Since both F and A are in the F chord, and since we used the F chord in measure 3, we can stay with it. Notice that the G comes on a weak, not a strong, beat of the measure. If it had come on the first beat, we might have needed a chord change. Play over the song fragment in Illustration 27, with the chords, and notice how the passing tone (G) sounds consonant.

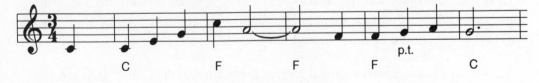

ILLUSTRATION 27

In measure 5, a change of chord is definitely required. There are three chords that contain the note G: I (CEG), iii (EGB), and V (GBD). The conservative, "safe" harmonization of any song is to go back to I whenever possible. Try all three chords and see which you like best in this measure. In measure 6, our choice is dictated to us; the only chord that contains both G and C is the I chord. Measure 7 obviously requires the I chord again, since all the melody notes are found in that chord.

Measure 8 cannot be harmonized with either the I chord (CEG) or the IV chord (FAC) satisfactorily. The only chord that contains both G and D is the V chord (GBD). The same chord can be used for measure 9, with the last note (C) serving as a passing tone. Measure 10 can also be harmonized by the V chord, using the C as another passing tone. Use the I chord for measures 11 and 12, and the harmonization is now complete. Illustration 28 shows the song and its harmonization.

ILLUSTRATION 28

This may not be the most exciting or interesting harmonization of the song we could devise, but it is solid, effective, and "safe." Notice that there are only four chord changes, and that each chord lasts for three measures (except for the beginning and ending). This balanced structure, with its stable, solid feel, well suits a folk song that has endured for centuries.

As a final project for this chapter, harmonize the melody in Exercise F on Worksheet #7, following the instructions given.

# WORKSHEET #7

## Exercise A

Harmonize the following melody in either thirds or sixths:

## Exercise B

Construct triads on each of these notes.

## Exercise C

1. If one of the chords in the following exercise is major, mark a capital *M* on the blank beneath the chord. If the chord is minor, mark a lowercase *m* on the blank. If the chord is diminished, mark a *d* on the blank.

2. Construct major chords on the first four notes below, and minor chords on the second four. Use accidentals on your added notes as needed.

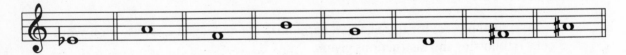

3. In the example below, the first chord (marked EXAMPLE) is the IV chord in the key of C. On each blank below, write the key in which that chord would have the indicated number.

EXAMPLE

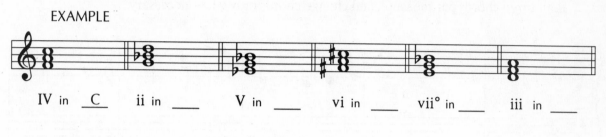

IV in __C__     ii in ___     V in ___     vi in ___     vii° in ___     iii in ___

## Exercise D

On the blank below each measure, write the number of the chord in accordance with the key signature.

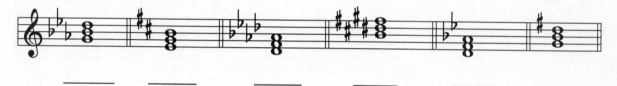

## Exercise E

On the bass staff below, write the indicated chords as block chords. Use the correct note value (half, quarter, etc.).

## Exercise F

On the bass staff, harmonize the following song in block chords. Use no more than three chords per measure, and change chords only when necessary.

# Chapter Seven

# Chord Progressions, Voice Leading, Four-Part Writing

## Chord Progressions

A *chord progression* occurs when you move from one chord to another chord that contains at least one different note. From CEG to EGC is *not* a chord progression, since the same notes are in both chords (even though the order is different). On the other hand, from CEG to CE-flatG *is* a chord progression, because at least one note is different in the second chord.

One of the most common chord progressions is based on chord roots a fourth apart. Such *root progressions* (chord progressions that are defined by the movement of the root tone) play a major role in all harmony. Let's examine a root progression "up a fourth" to see how it works. In Illustration 1A, the first chord is a C major chord, and the second chord is an F major chord. We can describe this progression as moving upward a fourth, from I (C) to IV (F). In Illustration 1A, it is easy to understand the concept because both triads are written in closed position. Illustration 1B is a little harder to follow since the notes of the C chord are written in an open position. Look carefully, however, and you will see that this, too, is a C chord (I) progressing to an F chord (IV). No matter what the position of either chord, so long as the first chord has CEG and the second has FAC, we say that a root progression up a fourth has occurred.

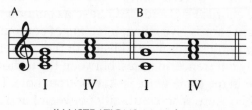

ILLUSTRATIONS 1A and 1B

Another very important root progression is the progression up a fifth, for example, from a C chord (I) to a G chord (V). In Illustrations 2A and 2B, we see two versions of a I-V progression, one from closed position, the other from open position. Imagine that these chords are written for three singers. Study these two versions carefully, especially Illustration 2B, to see how each voice moves from one chord to another.

ILLUSTRATIONS 2A and 2B

In Chapter 6, we wrote out the chords for "On Top of Old Smoky." Illustration 3 shows the harmonization we used for the song. Each of the chord progressions in the song is a root progression of a fourth or a fifth. From measure 1 to measure 2 (I to IV, C to F) is a progression up a perfect fourth. From measure 4 to measure 5 (IV to I, F to C) is a root progression back down a perfect fourth. From measure 7 to measure 8 (I to V, C to G) is an upward progression of a perfect fifth, and from measure 9 to measure 10 is a downward progression of a perfect fifth. In each case, the progression sounds strong and forceful.

ILLUSTRATION 3

What makes these progressions so strong? They have several attributes that help produce this effect. The first and most important is that all the notes in these chords agree with the key signature. There are no accidentals added to notes. Therefore, none of the notes suggests a change of key; the harmony notes constantly reinforce the sound of the key.

A second attribute strengthening these progressions is that in each progression there is one tone common to the two chords. The chords FAC and B-flatDF have a common tone of F; the chords FAC and CEG have a common tone of C. Using a tone common to two adjacent chords gives them a feeling of continuity or relatedness. Play the chord progressions in Illustration 4 and listen to them carefully. In each case, the first chord is I. The only difference, in notes, between the ii chord and the IV (here modified to keep the F in the same voice) is the bottom note. The careful listener will note, however, that while there is no continuity between I and ii, since every note in the first chord changes, there is a strong feeling of relationship between I and IV. This is because of the common tone these two chords share.

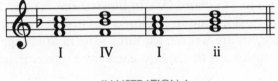

ILLUSTRATION 4

Odd though it seems, another attribute strengthening these progressions is the fact that two pitches change in each progression. In the key of F, the I-IV progression

requires changing A to B-flat and C to D (Illustration 5A). The I-V progression
requires changing F to E and A to G (Illustration 5B). If only *one* of these notes

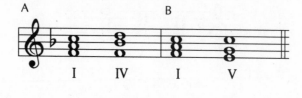

changed, the sense of movement from one chord to another would be much weaker.
For example, in Illustration 6A, compare the I-IV progression with the I-vi progression, which differs by only one note. The first progression has much more of a sense of
change than the second. In Illustration 6B, compare the I-V progression with I-iii.
Again, the sense of movement is much stronger when two voices change. Of all the

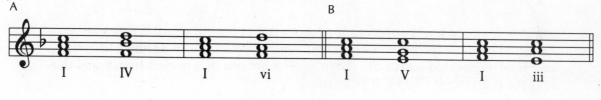

chord progressions possible in the major scale, only progressions of perfect fourths
and fifths have all three of the attributes listed above in common. Root progressions
of a second (for example, I-ii, I-vii°) require all three notes to change; progressions of
a third (for example, I-iii or I-vi) require that only one note change. Progressions of an

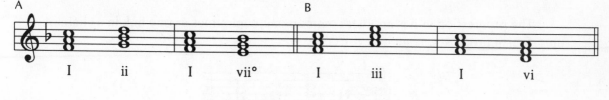

*augmented fourth*, by the way, are very unusual; normally, all three notes change and
accidentals are included.

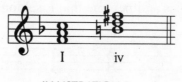

So far, we have referred to progressions in which one of the chords is the I chord.
Any root progression of a fourth or fifth will be equally strong, and others are quite

common. The progression ii-V, for example, often appears, especially in the three-chord progression ii-V-I.

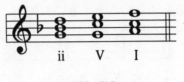

ILLUSTRATION 9

The progression iii-vi is also strong, even though both chords are minor. The progres-

ILLUSTRATION 10

sion IV-vii° almost never appears. One reason is that the vii° chord is a diminished chord and has little feeling of a key center. Another reason is that from 4 to 7 in a scale is an augmented fourth; the progression is not one of a perfect fourth, and thus lacks the characteristic "up-a-fourth" sound.

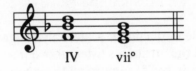

ILLUSTRATION 11

The progression vi-ii is another common one, sometimes as one link in a chain of up-a-fourth progressions such as vi-ii-V-I.

ILLUSTRATION 12

The progression vii°-iii is another one that is seldom used.

ILLUSTRATION 13

At this point, you should harmonize Exercise A on Worksheet #8 and have your teacher check your work.

## Voice Leading

It is most important that, as you write out chord progressions, you take special care with *voice leading*. Assume you have a progression of triads to be sung by three singers. One singer will perform all the lowest notes in the triads (the roots); a second will sing all the middle notes; and the last will sing all the highest notes. The way in which any one singer moves from one note to the next is what is meant by voice leading. Even in instrumental music, good, smooth voice leading is important. Let's illustrate the problem with two examples of voice leading, one bad, one good. If we write each triad in root position, then copy the parts on three separate staves, we might obtain the following:

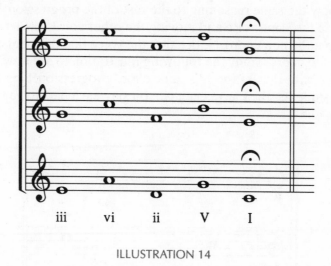

iii    vi    ii    V    I

ILLUSTRATION 14

Follow each part through from beginning to end. Each jumps wildly about by fourths and fifths, making it awkward and uncomfortable to sing or play on an instrument. Poor voice leading makes unsingable music, or unmusical singing.

Fortunately, the solution is simple. The trick is to move each note in the first chord (iii) the least possible distance to arrive at *any* of the three notes in the second (vi) chord. The iii chord (EGB) and the vi chord (ACE) share a common note—E. One of the three voices, therefore, can sing the E in both these chords. The G in the iii chord can move up a second to the A in the vi chord; similarly, the B in the iii chord can move to the C in the vi chord. The result is a smooth, very singable progression.

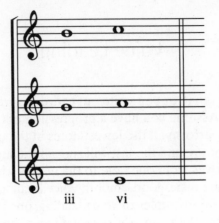

ILLUSTRATION 15

We can apply the same reasoning to the rest of the progression, by keeping common notes in the same voice and moving the other voices the least possible distance to fill out the new chord. Notice that the voice that does not change pitch will vary from chord to chord. Study the following illustration to see how this can work out; compare this with Illustration 14's same chord progression. Sing this progression with two other students. Then have each person sing each part to get the feel of good, smooth voice leading.

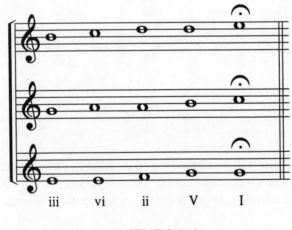

ILLUSTRATION 16

Now you should work Exercise B on Worksheet #8 and have your teacher check your work.

# Four-Part Harmonization

So far in our study of harmony, we have dealt with no more than three voices or instrumental parts at a time. Yet most written music has a minimum of four, and often even more, separate parts. In vocal music, pieces for mixed voices (male and female together) are usually scored for SATB, which stands for soprano, alto, tenor, and bass. Even with all-male or all-female ensembles, four-part writing is common—SSAA (first and second sopranos, first and second altos) or TTBB (first and second tenors, baritones, and basses). With instrumental music, one often finds pieces for string quartets (first and second violins, viola, and cello), clarinet quartets (first and second B-flat clarinets, E-flat alto clarinet, B-flat bass clarinet), or brass quartets of varying instrumentation (trumpet, French horn, trombone, and tuba; or first and second trumpets, trombone or French horn, and baritone or tuba). What is more, even pieces written for much larger instrumental groups, such as full band or orchestra, can often be reduced to four essential parts with several instruments playing each of the parts.

We can illustrate this using the short chorale in Illustration 17. If we score the

ILLUSTRATION 17

chorale for SATB choir, the result will look like Illustration 18. Sing this version through in class, and notice the voice leading in each of the parts. Examine the chorale itself carefully. When we write for four voice or instrument parts using triads, it is obvious that at least one tone must be doubled (that is, sung or played by two performers) in each chord. In the first chord, for example, the E-flat is doubled, appearing in both the bass and tenor voices. In the second chord, the A-flat is doubled (bass and alto); in the third chord, bass and tenor again have an E-flat; and so on.

Notice that the upper three voices (S, A, and T) are written with careful attention to voice leading. On the other hand, the bass bounds around in great, kangaroo-like leaps. This type of motion is more characteristic, and more acceptable, in the bass than in the upper three voices. Notice also that, of the upper three voices, no two adjacent voices are ever more than an octave apart, while the bass at one point plunges an octave and a fifth below the tenor. From all this, it is obvious that the voice-leading rules for the upper three parts don't apply nearly so strictly to the bass.

ILLUSTRATION 18

Now we can arrange the same chorale for eight wind instruments (Illustration 19). At the beginning of each instrument part is a letter that identifies the part as soprano, alto, tenor, or bass. Compare these parts with the same parts in the SATB score. Remember that certain parts have been transposed!

In this chorale, the bass is given the root of each chord. Bass parts tend to proceed by root movement, with certain exceptions. Therefore, they tend to be more active and widely spaced than other voice parts. The root of the first chord, I, is E-flat. The next chord, IV, has A-flat for a root. The third chord is another I, and the fourth chord, V, has a B-flat root. In each chord, the bass is given the root note. This is what is meant by the term *root movement*.

ILLUSTRATION 19

An important quality of smooth four-part writing is the principle of *contrary motion*, especially between the outer parts, the soprano and the bass. Examine just the two outer parts in Illustration 20 for a moment.

As the soprano moves upward from chord 1 to chord 2, the bass moves downward. From 2 to 3, the soprano moves downward while the bass moves upward. This series of moves clearly illustrates contrary motion. When one part moves, the other part moves in the opposite direction. The *distance* each part moves is not important; it is the *direction* that counts.

Another sort of tonal motion is illustrated by the soprano and bass in the change from chord 3 to chord 4. Here the soprano stays on the same note while the bass

ILLUSTRATION 20

moves downward. When one part moves in *either direction* while the other stays still, it is called *oblique motion*.

Still a third type of relative motion is illustrated by bass and soprano as they move from chord 9 to chord 10. Both parts move in the same direction here; this is called *similar motion*. This type of motion must be handled with great care if the end result is to sound smooth.

When you write or arrange a piece of music, you want the result to sound as smooth and professional as possible, without rough, awkward chord changes. When trying for good results, tonal motion is the critical factor. It has taken good composers and arrangers hundreds of years of experimenting to work out the principles of good voice leading and tonal motion, yet these principles can be stated in a few short sentences. The more closely you follow these principles, the more professional your results are likely to sound.

The first principle of tonal motion is that *contrary motion and oblique motion are always safe*. When moving from one chord to another, if any two voices move in opposite directions or obliquely, the progression of those two voices will sound smooth. Look once more at the original version of the chorale in Illustration 17. From chord 1 to chord 2 in this four-voice progression, we see all three types of tonal motion: contrary motion (S, or A, and B); oblique motion (T and B); and similar motion (S and A). Play each pair of parts separately and listen to the results. Then play all four parts on a keyboard instrument and listen for the smooth effect, especially when the motion of parts is either contrary or oblique.

The second principle of good tonal motion is that *similar motion must be treated very carefully*. What really matters is not what interval the progression begins with, but how it ends. Endings in thirds and sixths are safe; similar motion to either of those intervals will sound smooth. Similar motion to any other interval risks sounding rough and awkward. This is especially true of perfect fourths and fifths.

Play the progressions in Illustration 21 and listen carefully to the effect of each.

The first two interval progressions move by contrary motion; the second interval in each progression is approached smoothly and without awkwardness. The next two progressions move by oblique motion; again, they sound relatively graceful. The final

ILLUSTRATION 21

two progressions represent similar motion. The first progression ends on a third, and it sounds quite smooth. On the other hand, the next one ends in a perfect fourth; it sounds hollow and rough. Similar motion to fourths and fifths results in awkward-sounding music.

Such faulty progressions are easy enough to avoid when you are dealing with only two voices. The task is greatly complicated in four-part writing because you should avoid similar motion to fourths and fifths between *all possible pairs of voices*— S and A, S and T, S and B, A and T, A and B, and T and B. If similar motion between any of these pairs results in a perfect fourth or fifth, and most especially when it happens between bass and soprano, the sound will be awkward.

Let's return to the chorale to see how such problems can be avoided. In the first place, the two outer voices are taken care of by assuring that they move in contrary or oblique motion whenever possible. Since the bass is playing the roots of the chords, this part is not too flexible; it can move either up or down to the root of the next chord. If the bass goes upward at a given point and the soprano comes downward, the two inner parts are sometimes squeezed into a very small space, as in Illustration 22.

ILLUSTRATION 22

This illustration represents a revision of the first two chords of the chorale. To avoid similar motion to a perfect fourth (S and A), the alto must join either the soprano's note or the tenor's, producing a thin-sounding, three-note chord. While this is some-times necessary, it needn't happen here, as in Illustration 17 where the bass goes downward and the soprano upward, giving alto and tenor lots of breathing room.

Look at Illustration 17. In chord 1, the bass has the root of the chord and the soprano has the fifth; the third of the chord will be assigned to one of the other parts while the last part should double another part, probably the root. The tenor in this instance doubles the root an octave higher while the alto has the third; the chord is complete. In chord 2, the bass again has the root while the soprano now has the third of this new chord. The fifth of the chord, E-flat, can be carried over in the tenor from the previous chord. The alto now doubles the root, and the full chord is represented here as well.

Now let's check the tonal motion. Soprano and bass are in contrary motion; no problems here. The tenor moves obliquely with all other parts; again, no problems. The alto moves contrary to the bass (good), but in similar motion with the soprano. A quick check of these two parts shows that in the second chord they are a third apart. Since this is a smooth change, the whole progression works out well.

Now check the progression from chord 2 to chord 3. The bass and the soprano are in contrary motion; the tenor again moves obliquely to the other parts; the alto moves in similar motion with the soprano to another third. Check each of the other progressions in the chorale for yourself.

Once you have completed this study, you are ready to work Exercise C on Worksheet #8. From now on, in all the writing and arranging of music you do, you should check to see that the voice leading is correctly done. Later on, you may wish to write in a style that contradicts good voice-leading principles. It is most important at this point, however, that you master these principles before you abandon them. There is a difference between breaking the rules intelligently and writing out of ignorance. It is the difference between the craftsperson and the amateur.

## Exercise A

1. On the blank beneath each chord, write the chord number. Be sure to check the key signatures.

2. On the staff below, write out the chords that correspond to the numbers written below the measures. Again, check the key signatures carefully.

IV      vi      ii      V      iii

## Exercise B

In whole notes, write out the appropriate chord for each number below the staff. Apply good voice-leading principles in your work.

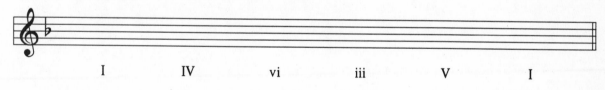

I      IV      vi      iii      V      I

## Exercise C

Harmonize the bass line below, adding three upper parts and illustrating good voice leading. All chords are, of course, in root position.

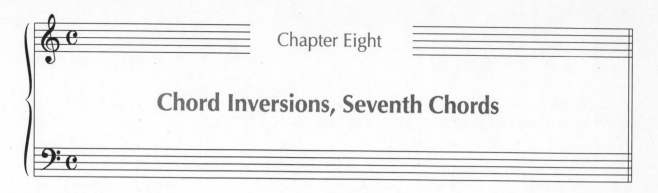

## Chapter Eight

# Chord Inversions, Seventh Chords

## Chord Inversion

As we have seen from the work in Chapter Seven, a triad will sound like the same triad regardless of the order, from lowest to highest, in which the notes are arranged. The C major triad (CEG) always sounds like the C major triad, whether it is spelled CEG, EGC, or GCE. It is this principle that makes good voice leading possible. Changing the order of the notes, from lowest to highest, is a process called *chord inversion*. The bass part may be used in inverted positions as well as in root position. We must use great care and special guidelines for writing inverted bass parts, however, because bass notes affect the sound of the chords more than any other voice. Poor bass movement can destroy the effectiveness of an otherwise strong harmonization.

Let's examine two versions of a piano arrangement of French composer Charles Gounod's piece entitled, "Lovely, Appear." We will only use the first eight measures of the piece. In Illustration 1, the bass has the root of each chord.

This arrangement is quite acceptable, if a bit "foursquare" and predictable. The voice leading in the upper parts is also good. Tenor and soprano exchange notes in measure 1, giving the appearance of movement without actually changing chord. The arrangement is satisfactory, if not brilliant.

Compare this with Gounod's own version in Illustration 2. The chords in this version are exactly the same as in the first version. In each chord marked with an X, however, the bass has some note of the chord other than the root. These are *inverted* chords.

Compare the bass parts of these two versions (Illustration 3). Each part spans an octave (C to C in the first version, D to D in the second). However, while the first version has jumps of seconds, fourths, and fifths, the second is more complex and scalewise. The other voices are nearly identical in the two versions; only the bass voices are quite different.

Play the two versions over again, and listen to the effect each achieves. The first version sounds like a solid processional tune, respectable and upright, virtuous and direct. The second version is much more ambiguous and indefinite, almost floating and

ILLUSTRATION 1

ILLUSTRATION 2

ethereal; it must be played slowly in a hushed manner, as if shouting and marching about might frighten away the "Lovely" whose appearance is summoned. This change, again, is the result of the modified bass part.

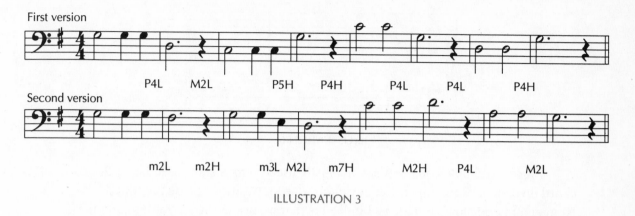

First version

P4L   M2L   P5H   P4H   P4L   P4L   P4H

Second version

m2L   m2H   m3L  M2L   m7H   M2H   P4L   M2L

ILLUSTRATION 3

There are three positions of triads—root position and two inversions—each of which has certain conventions of use that you should observe because they have proved to be most effective over centuries. Let's begin with chords in root position, that is, with the root in the bass. All of the C chords in Illustration 4 are in root position because, in each case, the bass note is C. This note alone determines whether a chord is in root position.

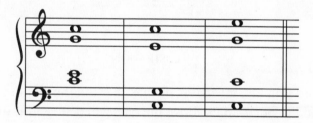

ILLUSTRATION 4

If the bass note is the third of the triad, the chord is said to be in *first inversion*. The chords in Illustration 5 are all first-inversion chords. Notice that, in these triads, no other part is given the third of the triad; this is a characteristic of first-inversion chords that we will discuss shortly.

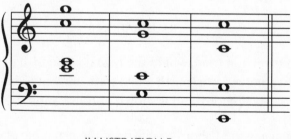

ILLUSTRATION 5

If the bass note is the fifth of the triad, the chord is said to be in *second inversion*. The chords in Illustration 6 are all chords in second inversion.

ILLUSTRATION 6

There is a simple code that is universally used by musicians to indicate these chord inversions. Remember that any chord in root position can be identified by a Roman numeral alone. F major—I indicates that we are in the key of F major, the bass has an F, and the other notes of the chord are a third above F (A) and a fifth above F (C), or some octave of those notes. We might write the chord as $I_3^5$, but there is no need to; the 3 and the 5 are assumed to be part of the I chord, as in Illustration 7.

ILLUSTRATION 7

When a chord is in first inversion, the bass has the third of the triad (A, in the F major chord), and the other notes above the bass will be C and F. In closed position, the F is now a sixth above the bass note, and the C is a third above. We might write the chord symbol as $I_3^6$; in practice, the third above the bass (C) is assumed and only the sixth is mentioned. The chord is labeled $I^6$, as in Illustration 8.

ILLUSTRATION 8

In the second inversion triad, where the bass has the fifth of the chord (C, in F major), the other two notes are a fourth and a sixth above the bass, respectively. The chord is referred to as a $I_4^6$ chord, and is shown in Illustration 9.

We have been using the I chord to illustrate the principle of chord inversion; but, in fact, *any* chord may be written in any inversion. Obviously, the other notes of the chord need not be precisely a fourth or sixth above the bass in order for it to be labeled a 6 or 6-4 chord. The numbers simply indicate the inversion of the chord, whether first or second, not the precise location of the other notes.

Let's reexamine "Lovely, Appear" in the Gounod arrangement, this time with the chord symbols marked beneath the notes (Illustration 10). One caution: In measure 7, the soprano changes to a dissonant note, creating a special chord that will be discussed later in this chapter.

For the time being, you should be careful to observe the following principles as you write inverted chords.

1. *In first-inversion chords, it is best to double a note other than the bass.* The root notes of chords in first inversion are weakened in sound, because one's ear tends to hear the bass note as the root. Doubling the bass, therefore, further weakens the basic color of the triad. Furthermore, if the bass is going up a step from the first inversion, doubling the bass often results in parallel octaves, which should be avoided (see Illustration 11).

2. *When using second-inversion chords, the bass note is commonly doubled*, especially when using the so-called cadential 6-4 progression, which often ends a phrase. The final V-I progression, or any comparable strong ending to a phrase, is

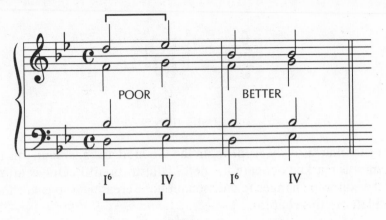

ILLUSTRATION 11

called a *cadence* (see Illustration 12A). Another common use of the 6-4 chord with doubled bass is in the auxiliary 6-4 progression, which sounds like the "A-men" ending of a hymn (see Illustration 12B).

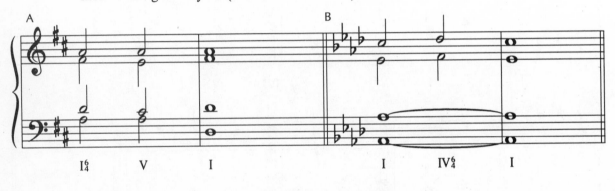

ILLUSTRATIONS 12A and 12B

3. As always, *let your ear be your guide.* Become aware of the ways in which successful and imaginative arrangers and composers use chords for color and expression. Listen carefully to many different pieces in many different styles. Try chords out with different voicings or different note doublings. Sometimes a small change makes a great difference in the sound of a chord or progression. Constantly check individual parts for smooth motion. Then pick the arrangement of the chords that suits you best and stick with it. On the other hand, if you later change your mind, don't be lazy: rewrite. That's why erasers are put on pencils. Always do the best work you can; it is *your* integrity on the line.

Using inverted chords gives you much more freedom within the parts than using strictly root position chords. It can help smooth out many sticky problems in individual parts. Inverting chords also makes your job much more demanding, for you must see to it that all the parts flow in a singable, logical manner. As you write music using chord inversions and using care with the voice leading, the process will gradually become more comfortable to you. It will then be less a matter of following burdensome rules than of creating interesting music.

You should test your command of chord inversions by working Exercise A on Worksheet #9. As always, have your teacher critique your results.

# Seventh Chords

During our discussion of harmonization so far, we have been working with triads. Skillful use of triadic harmony is essential for any arranger or composer, since the triad is the fundamental element in any traditional harmonization. Nonetheless, after a while, three-note chords begin to seem bland and colorless. We wish for something more dynamic and interesting in our palette of tonal color. The seventh chord is the most important source of that added interest, the hot sauce in our chili.

To define a seventh chord, let's first review the construction of a triad: a bass note is chosen and two other notes are added, a third and a fifth above the bass, respectively. These chords are symbolized by either numbers (ii, V) or letters (A, Dm), and they can be major, minor, diminished, or augmented. Sometimes chords are described as being built by the third-on-third method, since one begins with a bass note, adds a note a third above the first, and then adds another note a third above this second note (Illustration 13A).

ILLUSTRATIONS 13A and 13B

A seventh chord is built by taking the third-on-third process one step further; another third is added above the top note of the triad, as in Illustration 13B. The new note will be the one that naturally occurs in the scale. This is called a seventh chord because the new note is the seventh scale step above the root (Illustration 14). This

ILLUSTRATION 14

chord is indicated by the symbol $F^7$, or $I^7$ in the key of F major.

Seventh chords can be based on any note of any scale. Here are the seventh chords built on the steps of the D major scale:

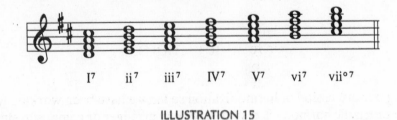

$I^7$     $ii^7$     $iii^7$     $IV^7$     $V^7$     $vi^7$     $vii°^7$

**ILLUSTRATION 15**

The sevenths add more color or spice to a harmonization because they have a great deal more dissonance than a triad. Notice that the sevenths in the above chords are sometimes *minor* sevenths (as in $ii^7$) and sometimes *major* sevenths (as in $IV^7$). This refers not to the mode of the chord, but to the interval of the seventh above the root.

Each of these seventh chords has a certain color or quality. The $I^7$ is a rich, thick-textured chord. The dissonance of the major seventh is tempered by the consonance of the other two notes, so that the chord sounds lush rather than edgy. The $ii^7$ is a very useful chord. It often leads to a V chord since it is a fourth below the V; adding the seventh makes the ii chord drive more powerfully toward a consonance. Adding the minor seventh interval to a minor triad creates an unstable sound.

The $iii^7$ is quite weak, just as the iii triad is, and for the same reason. Its intervals are like those of the $ii^7$ chord (that is, a minor triad with a minor seventh), and it can thus be used to lead to a vi chord. The $IV^7$ has the same interval structure as the $I^7$ (that is, a major triad with a minor seventh). It is not a frequently used chord except in certain styles of music, which will be discussed later.

The $V^7$ chord, on the other hand, is used a great deal. The minor seventh interval adds a strong dissonance to the V, giving it a great feeling of restlessness or motion. The $V^7$ chord is a commonly used version of the V chord. It is worth noting that the $V^7$ chord has all the notes of the vii° chord in its makeup. This is another reason why the vii° is so seldom used; it sounds like a $V^7$ chord with the root missing.

The $vi^7$ chord has little strength on its own. The main reason is that, like the vii° chord, it closely resembles another familiar chord, the I chord with an added sixth above the root. This chord, like the $I^7$ and $IV^7$, is frequently used in jazz and stage band arrangements. Finally, the $vii°^7$ is a weak, characterless chord unless altered; it has little function on its own.

Of all these chords, by far the most important for our present needs are the $ii^7$ and the $V^7$. Sevenths may be added to any chord at the discretion of the arranger, but ordinarily they are used simply to increase the sense of movement in certain chords. Notice the differences between the two progressions in Illustration 16. The seventh added in Illustration 16B gives more drive toward the final chord.

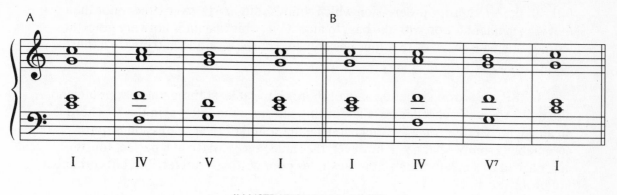

ILLUSTRATIONS 16A and 16B

Using the $V^7$ chord instead of the V chord may cause problems with voice leading. If so, a simple solution is available. The $V^7$ chord gets its characteristic sound from the combination of a major third interval above the root and a minor seventh interval above the root. The perfect fifth above the root can be omitted without changing the chord's character; in fact, you may have trouble telling if the fifth is included in the chord. Play the two progressions in Illustration 17: Does the lack of a fifth in the $V^7$ of the second progression make it sound different? Since the fifth is optional in the $V^7$

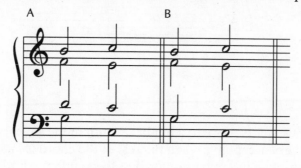

ILLUSTRATIONS 17A and 17B

chord, it is possible to omit it entirely. This may be of great help in improving voice leading. Study the progressions in Illustration 18, both of which include $V^7$ chords with the fifth of the chord present. In 18A, the tenor and bass move in parallel perfect

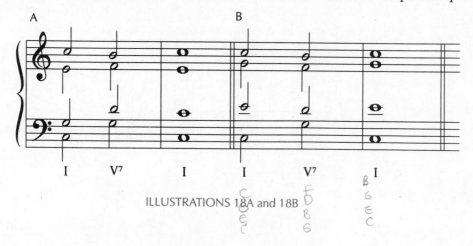

ILLUSTRATIONS 18A and 18B

fifths to the V[7] chord, a progression which sounds rough. Afterward, the tenor then moves in similar motion with the bass to an octave, which again is not very graceful writing. The final chord of 18A thus has only two notes, C and E, and makes a thin-sounding chord.

In 18B, the scoring is better, and all chords have at least three tones. Soprano and alto move to the V[7] chord in parallel fourths, but since the interval in the V[7] chord is an augmented, rather than a perfect, fourth, the sound of the progression is quite acceptable. From V[7] back to I, however, the same voices arrive at a perfect fourth, approached by similar motion. This illustrates poor writing—not terrible, but certainly not professional.

Now let's examine a progression omitting the fifth of the V[7] chord (Illustration 19). Here, the voice leading of each part is very smooth; only the bass and tenor are in

ILLUSTRATION 19

similar motion. These parts move to a minor seventh in the V[7] chord, which is dissonant by itself, but very acceptable when the rest of the chord is included. From V[7] to I these two parts are again in similar motion, but they end in a third (plus an octave, sometimes called a *tenth*), which is quite good.

Protestant church hymns use this type of harmonic progression constantly. Often the seventh of the V[7] chord is held back for a moment, then dropped into place just before the chord changes to I, as in Illustration 20. The effect is one of great finality,

ILLUSTRATION 20

and it reminds us that there are many, many ways to use these seventh chords imaginatively. We can delay the appearance of the seventh and increase the drama of a resolution. Or we might want to create a feeling of steady flow by playing the entire $V^7$ chord on the beat. Although it would hardly be standard practice, we might even end on a $V^7$ chord, creating a feeling of tension and incompleteness in the listener. The composer's taste and skill in using sounds are the final determinants of what is "good" or "bad" in writing music.

Sometimes seventh chords are strung together to make a sequence of dissonances leading to a final consonance, thus making the last chord sound even more final. The most common such sequence is $ii^7$-$V^7$-I. Voice leading works out very neatly here, although the fifth may have to be omitted in the $V^7$ chord, as in Illustration 21.

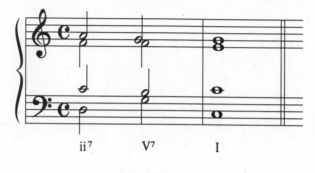

$$ii^7 \qquad V^7 \qquad I$$

ILLUSTRATION 21

Check your understanding of seventh chords by working Exercise B on Worksheet #9. Have your teacher check your work.

## Inversions of Seventh Chords

Of course, seventh chords can be inverted, just as any other chords. A first-inversion seventh chord is the same as a first-inversion triad, with the third of the chord in the bass, but with the seventh added. A second-inversion seventh chord has the fifth in the bass. When the seventh itself is in the bass, it becomes a *third-inversion* chord. Illustration 22 shows two third-inversion chords. Third-inversion chords usually appear in one of two situations: (1) as a passing tone when the bass has a scalewise line (Illustration 22), or (2) as a very dissonant seventh in a $V^7$ chord, which resolves to a I chord in first inversion (Illustration 23).

Seventh-chord inversions are marked differently from triad inversions. Root position chords are, of course, marked with an Arabic numeral 7 after the Roman chord numeral ($V^7$). When, for example, a V chord is written in its first inversion, it is indicated as a $V^6_5$ chord to distinguish it from the $V^6$ triad, since the notes making up the chord are a third, a fifth, and a sixth above the bass. In the second inversion, the notes are a third, a fourth, and a sixth above the bass. This can be called a $^6_4$ chord ($I^6_4$); by convention, it is referred to as a $^4_3$ chord ($I^4_3$). Finally, when the chord is in third

ILLUSTRATION 22

ILLUSTRATION 23

inversion, the other tones are a second, fourth, and sixth above the bass ($IV_2^6$); the shorthand version of this is simply $IV^2$.

This seems like quite a bit to keep track of, but there is a shortcut way to remembering the inversions of seventh chords. Examine this chart of seventh-chord inversions and their symbols.

| Chord | $V^7$ | $V_5^6$ | $V_3^4$ | $V^2$ |
|---|---|---|---|---|
| **Position** | Root | 1st inv. | 2nd inv. | 3rd inv. |

Just remember the number sequence, "7, 65, 43, 2," and you'll remember the chord symbols for seventh-chord inversions.

As a final project for this chapter, work Exercise C on Worksheet #9. Be especially careful with this assignment, as you have learned a lot of material in this chapter. Practice the assignments on manuscript paper before completing the final copy to hand in to your teacher.

# WORKSHEET #9

## Exercise A

1. Mark the chord number and its inversion on the blank below each chord.

2. Harmonize this melody with the given chords in the inversions indicated. Do not harmonize notes marked with an asterisk (*).

I     I   vii°⁶  I⁶  I   IV   V   I   I⁶₄   vi   IV   I⁶   V   vii°⁶ I   V

## Exercise B

Write the chord numbers beneath the chords in this exercise. Be sure to indicate added sevenths and inversions.

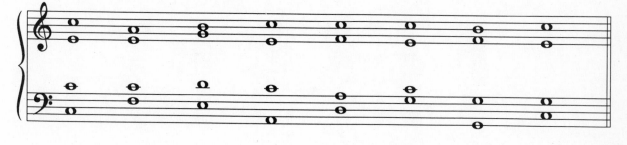

## Exercise C

Write in the numbers and inversions for the chords in this chorale. Account for each note in the chorale as either a chord tone or a passing tone (indicated by *PT*).

# Writing a Melody

What is a hit tune? It isn't necessarily a "top-40" song; they usually don't last out the year. No, a real hit tune is one that is popular and familiar for a long period of time, over a large territory, or both. By these standards, "Twinkle, Twinkle, Little Star" must rank near the top on the all-time hit parade; this simple little song has been around all of Europe and North America for over 300 years.

Composers such as Stephen Foster and George M. Cohan obviously understood what makes a good melody. So did Mozart, Tchaikovsky, Mendelssohn, Dvořák, and many others. March writers like John Philip Sousa, Karl King, and Henry Fillmore knew the secret. More recent popular songwriters such as Carol King, Andrew Lloyd Weber, and Stephen Sondheim are master tunesmiths.

The "secret" of writing successful melodies is really no secret at all, of course, nor is it any *one* thing. In this chapter we'll begin with a discussion of musical structure as one element of a successful melody.

## Structure

Suppose a composer has a nice idea for a melody and writes the idea down, perhaps sketching out some accompanying chords. After notating a phrase of melody, maybe sixteen measures long, he or she stops to ponder the composer's eternal problem: "What do I do next?" The choices are absurdly few. The songwriter can:

1. Do the same thing again.

2. Do something different.

3. Do the same thing in a different way.

The entire composition will evolve from a series of such choices that are made as the composer goes along. The longer the piece is, the more careful he or she must be about these decisions because of the greater risk of boring or confusing the audience.

Let's examine "Twinkle, Twinkle, Little Star" (Illustration 1) to see how it treats the problem of what to do next.

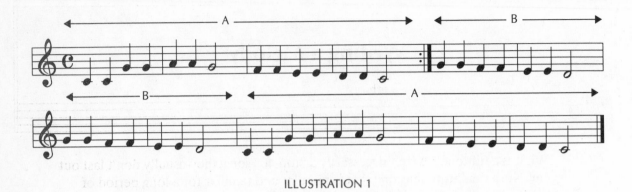

ILLUSTRATION 1

The basic melody (labeled A) is heard, and (in this version) is immediately repeated. This is followed by a new melody, B, which is only half the length of A, and is itself repeated. The piece concludes with the return of melody A. "Twinkle, Twinkle, Little Star" follows the pattern AABBA. This is its *form*.

Every melody follows a formal pattern, but not all of them are the same. The song "America," for instance, has two phrases; its form is AB (Illustration 2). "London

ILLUSTRATION 2

Bridge Is Falling Down" has the form ABAC (Illustration 3).

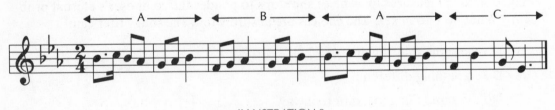

ILLUSTRATION 3

"The Marines' Hymn" has the form AABA (Illustration 4). "Row, Row, Row Your Boat" has an ABCD form (Illustration 5).

The same song may be diagrammed differently by different people. For example, "Twinkle, Twinkle, Little Star" is sometimes sung without repeating the first phrase. Also, since phrases tend to be of the same length, the two B phrases can be combined

ILLUSTRATION 4

ILLUSTRATION 5

into one B, and the shorter, repeated sections can be indicated by lowercase b's below the capital B, as in Illustration 6. When analyzed this way, our song has the form ABA.

ILLUSTRATION 6

Frequently, one phrase of a song will be *nearly* identical to another except for a few notes, usually at the end of the phrase. The famous melody from Beethoven's "Choral Symphony" illustrates such differences in phrases, as can be seen in Illustration 7. The first two phrases are essentially the same, except for the last three notes. To indicate the difference in phrases, we can use a small numeral 1 beside the A, to represent the second phrase. The third phrase will be indicated with a B, of course, giving us A-A1-B. How would the final phrase be indicated?

The *function* of a melody may help determine its form. "Row, Row, Row Your Boat," for instance, is a round; several voices sing different phrases at the same time. If any two phrases are the same, then two voices will have the same part, and the character of the round will be weakened. In a round, once the second voice has started singing, each phrase should be different from the others.

The *length* of the melody is another consideration. The longer a melody is, the more important it becomes to repeat a section. A short tune like "Row, Row, Row Your Boat" (16 beats long) can be remembered easily. Longer ones, like "Swanee

ILLUSTRATION 7

River"—at 64 beats, four times the length of "Row, Row, Row Your Boat"—must have much repetition for the average person to remember them. The formal structure of "Swanee River" is A-A1-B-A1.

A third factor that affects a melody's form is the extent to which it remains in, or varies from, one *key*. (The subject of key changes will be discussed at length in other chapters.) Short songs usually stay in one basic key throughout; they are too short to permit a modulation (change of key). Longer songs may need more variety to keep up the listener's interest level. Examine the arrangement of "America, the Beautiful" in Illustration 8. The form is A-A1-B-C, which allows for quite a bit of variety by itself. The song also changes key in measure 6 (to G), then returns to the original key in measure 8. Notice that in measure 7 there is a $D^7$ chord, which is the dominant chord in G major. If the song did *not* modulate to G in measure 6, the chord would be a $d^7$ (ii in C major). Try both the $D^7$ and the $d^7$ chords here and see how they sound. The $d^7$ just isn't the right chord.

Any successful melody, however, must have a balance between variety and unity. There has to be some strong unifying element to the song or it will sound like a collection of phrases from four different songs. In "America, the Beautiful," unity is obtained by the rhythm. Notice that the rhythm for the first phrase is used in the other three phrases. This is called an *isorhythm* (*iso* means one), and we say that the song is *isorhythmic*. Some other songs that are isorhythmic are "Twinkle, Twinkle, Little Star" and "My Darling Clementine." Can you think of more?

The following principles apply to the formal structure of melodies:

1.  The shorter the song, the less the need for repetition. If the song is a round, there should be no repetition. In longer melodies, repetition is needed.

ILLUSTRATION 8

2. Many different patterns of phrases can be found, even in simple songs. Formal structures using one, two, three, or even four phrases are common. Some of these patterns, and the songs that illustrate them, are the following:

| | |
|---|---|
| AA1BA1—"Swanee River" | AA1BC—"America, the Beautiful" |
| ABAC—"London Bridge" | ABCD—"Are You Sleeping?" |
| ABCA— "Sweet Betsy from Pike" | AB—"On Top of Old Smoky" |

Test your understanding of this material by completing Exercise A on Worksheet #10, identifying the forms of these two melodies. Have your teacher check your work.

## Motif

Now let's take a single phrase apart to see what makes it tick. Let's begin by playing "Name That Tune." Play each of the patterns of tones in Illustration 9 in a steady, even rhythm; see if you can guess what song each tonal pattern represents. Answers may be found at the end of the chapter.

ILLUSTRATION 9

Assuming that you got them all right, what is there about these patterns that gives the tune away? The answer is that each tonal pattern is strongly associated with one song and almost no other. Play them again and see if you can imagine any other song using the same pattern. Perhaps you can, but there are not many.

We'll carry the test one step further. The rhythm patterns in Illustration 10 apply to the songs in Illustration 9, but they are in different order. Two have six notes and two have four notes. Try to match the rhythms with the tonal patterns.

ILLUSTRATION 10

Each rhythm pattern is characteristic of one song, almost to the exclusion of any other song. The rhythm patterns and tonal patterns, alone or in combination, make up what is called a *motif*. Motifs are the short, characteristic "signatures" of melodies.

Good strong melodies are easy to remember, largely because they repeat a motif over and over. Some songs consist of little else *but* a motif. In the song "Skip to My Lou," Illustration 11, measures 1 and 2 make up the motif. Measures 3 and 4 repeat

ILLUSTRATION 11

the motif a step lower, while measures 5 and 6 are identical with 1 and 2. Only measures 7 and 8 are really different. The folk song "Shoo, Fly, Don't Bother Me" works the same way.

Most melodies consist of one or two motifs. A good example is the song "Maryland, My Maryland," found in Illustration 12. The opening motif (marked A), which resembles "Here comes the bride," is immediately repeated on higher pitches. The second motif (marked B) contrasts with the vigorous A motif. The whole first phrase is

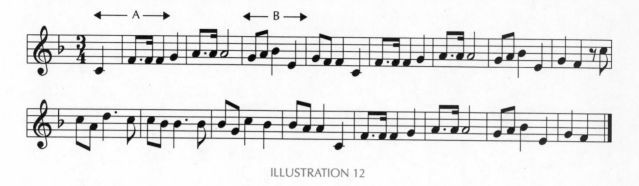

ILLUSTRATION 12

repeated (A-A) and then followed by a B section based on the B motif. The melody returns to the A phrase at the end.

A good motif is strong in rhythm and tonal motion because it is often varied within a song, rather than being repeated note for note. In Illustration 12, the second appearance of the motif (measure 2) has the same rhythm and the same upward motion as the first, but where the first appearance goes up a perfect fourth (measure 1), the second goes up only a major second (measure 2). The second statement is analogous to, rather than identical with, the first. Nonetheless, we easily recognize the similarity and understand that the second measure is just a variation on the first.

Sometimes a motif is slightly changed just to fit a change of chord in the song. In the Mexican folk song "La Cucaracha," presented in Illustration 13, we can see this type of change. The motif (first five notes) outlines the G chord at the beginning, but

ILLUSTRATION 13

when it appears in measures 4 and 5 it has been altered to fit the notes of the $D^7$ chord.

A motif may be recognizable even though it has been drastically changed. In Illustration 14, the melody is an old barbershop quartet song, "Sweet Genevieve." The motif in this song (the first four notes) features a dotted-eighth-and-sixteenth-note rhythm and a rather chromatic series of notes. In notes 1 to 4 the series skips up a sixth and moves upward. The next four notes (5 to 8) also feature the rhythm and the

ILLUSTRATION 14

chromatic nature of the notes, but the direction here is downward and all in half steps. We identify these two figures as variants of the same motif *because* of the similarities and *in spite* of the differences.

Now examine the rest of Illustration 14, observing how the motif is used in other places. Which parts are similar to the first four notes, and which are similar to the second four?

Composers of both art music and popular tunes make great use of motifs and often find interesting things to do with them. Sometimes they stretch a motif out over twice as much time, as in Illustration 15A, a process called *augmentation*. Sometimes they squeeze them into half the time of the original motif, as in Illustration 15B. This is called *diminution*.

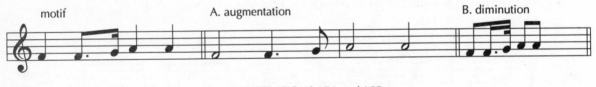

ILLUSTRATIONS 15A and 15B

Tchaikovsky, the popular Russian composer, used diminution of a motif quite cleverly in his Third Symphony. The low instruments play the motif in normal note values. When they are halfway through, the high instruments play it in diminution, making it sound as if they were running to catch up (see Illustration 16).

ILLUSTRATION 16

Sometimes a motif is *inverted*, or turned upside down. The German master Johannes Brahms wrote a lovely "Intermezzo" for piano (Op. 118, no. 2) that uses the motif in Illustration 17A. In measure 35, Brahms introduces a figure (Illustration 17B) that at first sounds like a new idea. This turns out to be an inverted form of the origi-

ILLUSTRATIONS 17A and 17B

nal motif. Where the original goes down a second and then up a third, the inversion goes up a second and down a third, and so on.

Some melodies use one main rhythmic motif at points throughout the composition. Notice how the dotted-eighth-and-sixteenth-note pattern dominates "The Battle Hymn of the Republic" (Illustration 18).

ILLUSTRATION 18

Other melodies, such as "Sourwood Mountain," have two strong and contrasting ideas (Illustration 19). Here the ideas alternate at two-measure intervals. Other such melodies are "Swing Low, Sweet Chariot," "All Night, All Day," and the sea chantey "Blow the Man Down." See if you can think of others.

One of the secrets to a good melody is a good strong motif. If you invent a strong motif, your melody nearly composes itself. We can illustrate the process by writing a song. Let's begin with a motif, simple in tonal motion, with a vivid rhythm pattern, as in Illustration 20. Next, decide on the formal structure you want to use. Try out two or

ILLUSTRATION 19

ILLUSTRATION 20

three patterns: AABA, AABB, ABAB, and so on—to see which one fits your ideas best. Keep in mind that you want a lot of repetition of your motif. Remember also that the B section should differ substantially from the A, and that it will probably be less forceful.

For the first phrase, start with the motif. Use it twice in the phrase. Change the pitch of the second occurrence to keep it from being too static. One solution might be similar to Illustration 21. Next, we will repeat the phrase, ending on *do* rather than on *mi*, as in Illustration 22.

ILLUSTRATION 21

ILLUSTRATION 22

For a B phrase, we'll use something less vivid, but we'll sneak the motif into the second half of the phrase, as in Illustration 23. Now you must decide how to finish the piece. Should you repeat A, repeat B, or invent a new phrase, C, to end the song? Illustration 24 provides two endings; you decide which you like better.

ILLUSTRATION 23

ILLUSTRATIONS 24A and 24B

Now that you see how simple it is, compose your own melody, using the previous steps as a guide (Worksheet #10, Exercise B). Don't be afraid to change things if you aren't satisfied. Also, don't be concerned if your first effort isn't a masterpiece. You learn by writing, and once you get the hang of it, you'll improve rapidly on your other attempts.

## Melodic Shape

The last aspect of good melody writing that we need to consider is melodic shape, or contour. Let's begin by considering *shape* in the visual arts. What do you think the picture in Illustration 25 represents?

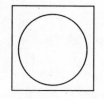

ILLUSTRATION 25

You might have said a hole, or a ball, or an orange, or Earth floating in space; all these answers (and many others) could be correct. In a more abstract sense, you might say that it symbolizes completeness, or self-sufficiency, or restfulness, or solidity. These answers are equally correct.

Now look at Illustration 26.

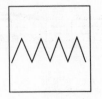

ILLUSTRATION 26

This picture could represent mountains, saw teeth, or ocean waves; it could symbolize regularity, or anxiety, or tension, or discord. Both these pictures could represent or symbolize many other things as well. The point is that they are *basic shapes* or *designs*. They can represent or symbolize a wide variety of objects or emotional states.

Just as there are standard visual shapes, there are standard melodic shapes as well. Let's consider a well-known melody and see how it represents a standard melodic shape (Illustration 27). The song consists of four phrases, has a phrase struc-

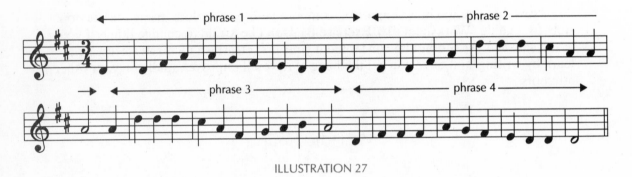

ILLUSTRATION 27

ture of A-A1-B-A2, and features the motif "*do-mi-sol.*" There is a strong isorhythmic motif throughout the song, shown in Illustration 28.

ILLUSTRATION 28

Let's carry the analysis a bit further. Phrase 1 begins and ends on *do*; phrase 2 begins on *do* but ends on *sol*; phrase 3 begins and ends on *sol*; and phrase 4 begins and ends on *do*. Furthermore, the range of notes in phrase 1 (from lowest to highest note) is a fifth, *do-sol*; for phrase 2, the range is an octave, *do-do*; for phrase 3, it is a sixth, *mi-do*; and for phrase 4, a fifth, *do-sol*, as in phrase 1. All this is summarized in Illustration 29.

Finally, each phrase has its own characteristic way of moving by step or by skip. Phrase 1 goes upward by skip and then downward by step (up the chord, down the scale). Phrase 2 skips up the chord for an octave, then comes down halfway, by step

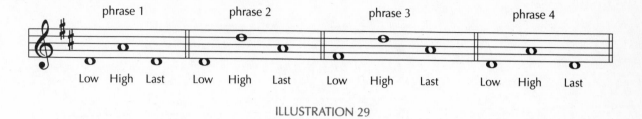

ILLUSTRATION 29

and skip. Phrase 3 begins with an upward skip, then moves by step and skip downward, and finally up by step, in a complex series of moves. Phrase 4 skips upward and returns by step.

Reduced to its simplest pattern, this type of melodic contour describes a large arc, or rainbow, over its four phrases, as can be seen in Illustration 30.

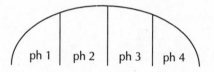

ILLUSTRATION 30

Other songs with similar melodic contours are "America, the Beautiful," "Frère Jacques," and "Down in the Valley." Can you think of still others?

It is easy to see why rainbow melodies often begin and end with A phrases. These songs have great strength and stability and are easily remembered because of the symmetry of their structures and the dramatic shape of their melodic contours.

Another typical melodic shape might be called the rocket. The rocket melody begins with a rapid climb upward and then meanders down from there. A good example of this form is Illustration 31, "On Top of Old Smoky."

ILLUSTRATION 31

We can see how the rocket effect occurs by analyzing the two phrases for their first and last notes, and their ranges, as in Illustration 32. Other songs that have a rocket contour are "Leaving Old Texas," "Twinkle, Twinkle, Little Star," and "The Ash Grove." Each of these songs tends to ascend quickly by skip and to descend by step.

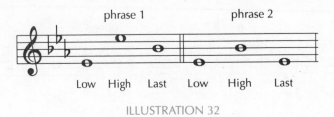

ILLUSTRATION 32

Certain other songs begin with a downward scale, and oscillate usp and down throughout the song. The familiar Christmas carol "Joy to the World" (Illustration 33) illustrates this type. This interesting melody has five phrases, two of which (phrases 3

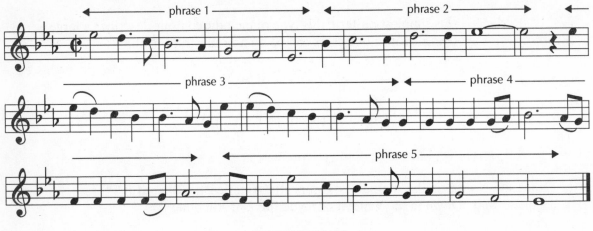

ILLUSTRATION 33

and 4) contain balancing half-phrases that are alike. Unlike the typical rocket melody, "Joy to the World" returns to its highest note several times. Other oscillating melodies are "The Streets of Laredo," "Away in a Manger," and the Creole song "Michie Banjo."

Some oscillating songs have ascending scales at their beginnings. One such melody is found in Illustration 34, "Long, Long Ago." Notice how much of this song

ILLUSTRATION 34

moves stepwise, rather than skipwise. Other songs of this type are "Row, Row, Row Your Boat," "Home, Sweet Home," and "Joshua Fit the Battle of Jericho."

Still other songs are based on ascending or descending chord patterns. Songs like those in Illustration 35 are based on ascending chord patterns. Other songs, like those

ILLUSTRATION 35

in Illustration 36, are based on descending chords.

ILLUSTRATION 36

Once in a while, a melody's contour will be influenced by the use of *text painting*; that is, music in which the notes illustrate the words of the song. In Illustration 37, the melody illustrates the text. The word "high" is sung on the highest note of the phrase, and the word "low" is sung on the lowest note. In Illustration 38, "Sweet and Low,"

ILLUSTRATION 37

the melody suggests the waves that are described by the words. In Illustration 39,

ILLUSTRATION 38

"Rockabye, Baby," the melody "rocks" back and forth over a range of a ninth, and gently swings in a ⁶⁄₈ meter.

Rainbows and rockets, scales and chords are all common melody shapes. Of course, there are many, many songs that don't follow any of these procedures. There are still other melody shapes not discussed here. For example, a song like "Bow, Belinda" goes alternately higher and lower than the starting note. A song like "Red River Valley" wanders back and forth within an octave before settling on the tonic.

Rock-a-bye, ba-by in the tree-top, When the wind blows, the cra-dle will rock.

When the bough breaks, the cra-dle will fall, and down will come ba-by, cra-dle and all!

ILLUSTRATION 39

Most good songs have their own distinctive personalities and shapes, although they are similar to other songs in some ways.

Here are some general principles of melodic shape which apply to most strong, memorable tunes. Keep these principles in mind when you create your own melodies; it will help you to write more vigorous, interesting tunes.

1. A good tune needs a strong motif that appears several times within the song. If a melodic motif is not used, a rhythmic one is even more important to provide melodic unity.

2. The tune should have a simple structure. It should feature some repetition, as in AABA, AABB, or AABC. Sometimes you can make the song more interesting by using an unusual structure like ABBA.

3. Melodies to be sung should have a range no greater than an eleventh (i.e., an octave plus a fourth). "The Star Spangled Banner" has a range of a twelfth, and most people find it to be at the limits of their vocal range.

4. Songs, or short melodies for instruments, should stick closely to the basic key, with diatonic notes on all strong beats and with few accidentals throughout. A longer melody may have more accidentals, and perhaps even a brief modulation.

5. Nearly all songs begin on a note of either the I or the V chord in the key. For now, make it a rule to end on the tonic note.

Principles such as these may be ignored, but only when the composer has a command of the art of writing music. For now, try to write good melodies "by the book." Later, you should experiment with different ideas.

These are some of the secrets of good tunesmithing: strong structures with repetition, a vivid motif, and an overall shape that gives drama to the melody. You are now ready to work Exercise C on Worksheet #10.

Answers to song-matching exercise at beginning of chapter: 1. "Star Spangled Banner," 2. "Silent Night," 3. "America," 4. Beethoven's *Symphony No. 5.*

## Exercise A

Identify the forms of the two songs below. Phrases end at the asterisks (*).

1. _____

2. _____

## Exercise B

Compose your own melody, beginning with a strong motif.

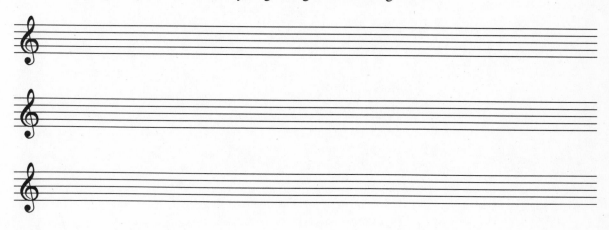

**Exercise C**

Compose a song using the rainbow, the rocket, or the scale shape.

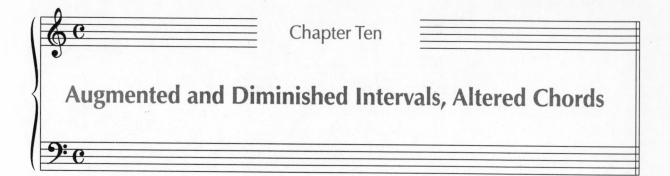

## Chapter Ten

# Augmented and Diminished Intervals, Altered Chords

In earlier chapters, we described scale intervals as major, minor, or perfect. Chords based on those intervals were either major or minor, except for the special case of the vii chord. We described it as "diminished," and then passed it over at the time. In this chapter, we will examine two unusual scale intervals, look at the vii chord again, and discover some special chords that these things suggest.

## Augmented and Diminished Intervals

All but one of the fourth intervals in a major scale are perfect fourths. In the C major scale, C to F is a perfect fourth; so is D to G, E to A, G to C, A to D, and B to E. Each of these intervals comprises five half steps. This will be true for the comparable intervals in any major scale, regardless of key. The one exception is the interval from 4 up to 7 (F up to B); this interval spans three whole steps, or six half steps. The distance between notes 4 and 7 in *any* major key is called an *augmented* ("added to") fourth. Any fourth with six half steps between its notes is an augmented fourth.

An inverted fourth becomes a fifth. All the fifths in the descending major scale are perfect—C down to F, B down to E, A to D, G to C, E to A, D to G—except for F down to B. A perfect fifth comprises seven half steps, but F to B comprises only six half steps. The interval F down to B (or 4 down to 7 in *any* key) is called a *diminished* ("made smaller") fifth. Any fifth with six half steps between its notes is a diminished fifth.

Augmented fourths and diminished fifths occur within the natural scale; however, by using accidentals, we can augment any fourth or diminish any fifth. Let's consider fourths first. Again using the C major scale as a model, we can augment the C-to-F interval in one of two ways. Remember that the trick is to add one more half step to the basic interval. We can do this by raising the F, or we can make an augmented fourth by lowering the C. These are shown in Illustration 1. In each case, we use an accidental to form the interval.

Once this is understood, it is obvious that any perfect fourth may be augmented in the same ways. Examine Illustration 2 to see how this can apply to intervals of the C major scale.

ILLUSTRATION 1

ILLUSTRATION 2

In other keys, a natural may be used to raise or lower a note to produce an augmented fourth, as in Illustration 3. What is needed in each case is to add an extra half step to a perfect fourth.

ILLUSTRATION 3

Doubtless you have already grasped that the same sort of procedure will produce diminished fifths. What is needed is to reduce a perfect fifth by one half step. Illustration 4 shows a number of diminished fifths in various keys.

ILLUSTRATION 4

Fourths may be diminished, and fifths may be augmented, by a similar process: either reduce by a half step to diminish or add a half step to augment. Illustration 5 presents a number of diminished fourths and augmented fifths.

diminished fourths                    augmented fifths

ILLUSTRATION 5

Perfect octaves, too, may be augmented or diminished by adding or subtracting a half step. A word of caution here; it is important that we begin with a *written octave* to augment or diminish the interval. A diminished octave, such as C to C-flat, sounds exactly like a major seventh (C to B), but it is treated differently in terms of harmonic progression. An augmented octave (C to C-sharp) *sounds* like a minor ninth (C to D-flat), but it, too, is treated differently in harmonic progression. This confusing business will, we hope, become clearer later in this book. Study the augmented and diminished octaves in Illustration 6.

ILLUSTRATION 6

Major intervals, like perfect intervals, may also be augmented (but not diminished). From C to D-sharp is an augmented second; from G to B-sharp is an augmented third; from B-flat to G-sharp is an augmented sixth; and from A-flat to G-sharp is an augmented seventh. In each case, the augmented interval is one half step larger than its major form. Illustration 7 shows various augmented seconds, thirds, sixths, and sevenths. Remember that if you raise a minor interval by a half step you

ILLUSTRATION 7

produce a major interval, not an augmented minor one; if you lower a major interval by a half step you get a minor one, not a diminished major one.

Making minor intervals a half step smaller produces diminished intervals. B up to C-flat is a diminished second; A-sharp up to C is a diminished third; D-sharp up to B-flat is a diminished sixth; G-sharp up to F is a diminished seventh. Illustration 8 presents a number of diminished seconds, thirds, sixths, and sevenths.

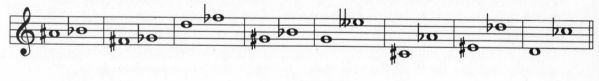

ILLUSTRATION 8

The alert student will likely be puzzled by all of this. A diminished second *sounds* like a perfect unison; a diminished sixth *sounds* like a perfect fifth. Why not just write the sounds-like interval, and forget about all this other business? The answer is that we are moving from writing music all in one key to writing music that changes key, often frequently. These ambiguous intervals become useful in the process of changing key. Once more, this should become clear in later chapters.

At this point you should do Exercise A on Worksheet #11. As always, have your teacher check your work.

# Altered Chords

In Chapter 6, we discussed the vii chord, describing it as a diminished chord that is made by placing a minor third atop another minor third. The notes above the root are a minor third and a diminished fifth, respectively. Any chord with this structure, not just the vii chord in a major key, will be a diminished triad. Illustration 9 shows a number of diminished chords.

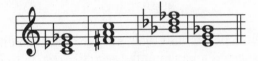

ILLUSTRATION 9

The chords in Illustration 9 are made by adding accidentals (flats, sharps, or naturals) to obtain the correct interval. When we modify any chord by adding accidentals, it becomes an *altered* ("changed") chord. Any chord that has its structure changed by one or more accidentals is an altered chord.

Turn back to Chapter 9 and study measures 6 and 7 of Illustration 8, "America, the Beautiful." The key at the beginning of the song is C major; however, in measure 6 the song suddenly changes to the key of G major. As you know, G major has a key signature of F-sharp; no change is made to the signature at the beginning of the line, however, since the key change is only temporary, and the song quickly returns to C major.

Measure 7 has four notes with accidentals before them: A-sharp and C-sharp on beat 1, and F-sharp on beats 3 and 4. These are altered chords. The chord on beat 1 has the notes G, A-sharp, and C-sharp. At first glance, this may seem like some exotic form of augmented chord. To find the truth, convert the A-sharp and C-sharp to their enharmonic equivalent notes, B-flat and D-flat. Now the chord is spelled GB-flatD-flat; it is a diminished triad based on G. Why weren't these notes written as flats, then? On beat 2 the chord is GBD, a major triad. Writing A-sharp and C-sharp is less confusing than cancelling B-flat and D-flat with naturals on beat 2. This illustrates one use of a diminished triad—to add some variety and color to a diatonic song.

The F-sharps on beats 3 and 4 have a different purpose. Suppose, for a moment, that the song is in the key of G. Measure 6 is all on the G chord; I in the key of G. The chord on beat 2 of measure 7 is also a I chord in G. The chord on beat 3 of measure 7 is a D-major chord with an added ninth; on beat 4, it is a D-major 7 chord. In the key of G, the D-major chord is the V chord. In other words, the chord progression from beat 2 of measure 7 is I-V$^9$-V$^7$ in the key of G. We have temporarily changed key to the key of G, and we have a I-V$^7$ progression in that key.

Now look at the first chord in measure 8. This is a G chord with a minor seventh added. The chord progression in measures 6 through 8 is I-V$^7$-I in G (ignoring the diminished chord and the ninth for the moment); but the G$^7$ chord in measure 8 is *also* the V$^7$ chord in the original key of C. In other words, at that point we are returning to the original key.

This is one example of how an altered chord can help change from one key to another; we will discuss this process at greater length in the next chapter. We have also seen how diminished chords are used to produce special color effects in a song.

One very useful form of the diminished chord is the *diminished seventh* chord, in which a diminished seventh above the root is added to a diminished triad (Illustration 10). All the intervals of this chord are minor thirds, leaving no pitch to serve as a key center. Beethoven used this chord effectively in his "Pathétique" Piano Sonata Op. 13

ILLUSTRATION 10

to heighten the drama at the very beginning of the work. Illustration 11A shows how he might have written the first measure using a i$^6_4$ chord in place of the diminished seventh. Compare this with Illustration 11B, which is what Beethoven actually did write. The diminished seventh is indicated by the chord number followed by two small

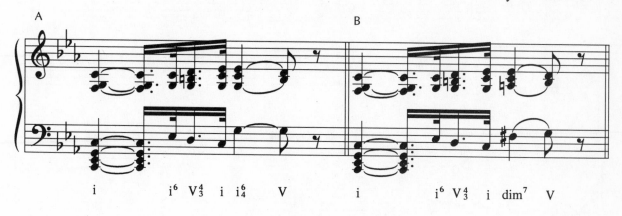

ILLUSTRATIONS 11A and 11B

zeroes, one above the other: vii$^\circ_\circ$. In silent film days, the pianist used diminished seventh chords in succession to represent impending disaster, as when the train was about to run over Little Nell. (See Illustration 12 for an example.)

Still another interesting use of the diminished seventh appears in Handel's *Messiah*, in the aria "He was despised" (Illustration 13). Here, the key is E-flat major, but for a moment Handel shifts to E-flat minor, harmonized by a diminished seventh chord, ACE-flatG-flat. This chord resolves to a V$^2$ chord and returns immediately to the major mode.

ILLUSTRATION 12

ILLUSTRATION 13

Because of its dissonant sound and lack of a key center, the diminished seventh chord is a wonderful means of modulating (changing) from one key to another.

Let's return to the augmented triad to see how it may be used effectively. Scott Joplin used an augmented chord to harmonize a chromatic passing tone in his rag called "The Entertainer." Illustration 14 is the beginning of the first melody in the rag; the D-sharp creates an augmented chord.

ILLUSTRATION 14

Like diminished seventh chords, augmented chords are ambiguous in key, and therefore are rather dissonant. When used in a series, they produce a floating, unstable effect with no tonal center, as in Illustration 15. Augmented chords are indicated by a

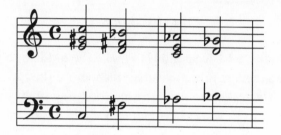

ILLUSTRATION 15

plus sign following the chord's numeral (I+). If you think you understand the above, do Exercise B on Worksheet #11 and have your teacher check your work.

## Change of Mode

As we have seen from the Handel example above, some altered chords result from a simple change of mode (major to minor or minor to major) in a piece of music. Certain Romantic-era composers, such as Dvořák, often stated a motif in major, then immediately restated it in minor. The excerpt in Illustration 16 comes from Dvořák's Symphony No. 9, *From the New World*.

ILLUSTRATION 16

Baroque-era composers often ended minor-key pieces on a major chord, raising the third of the last chord. This effect was so common that it had a name, the "tierce (third) de Picardy" (teerce deh PICK-ar-dee). We can see this at the end of Bach's famous "Little G-Minor Fugue" in Illustration 17.

ILLUSTRATION 17

Mozart sometimes used accidentals to make the mode of a piece ambiguous. Illustration 18 shows the last four measures (just before the *da capo*) of the third movement of *Eine Kleine Nachtmusik*, written for string orchestra. Notice how the chromatic melody seems to waver between major and minor mode. An altered third

ILLUSTRATION 18

of a chord is indicated in Roman numerals by changing from lower- to uppercase, or vice versa. Lowercase numerals, of course, indicate minor chords whereas uppercase indicate major chords. The progression i-iv-V$^7$-I indicates that the final chord has a tierce de Picardy; I-IV-V$^7$-i indicates a minor chord ending.

Some accidentals appear because the V chord is always major, even in a minor key, and requires an altered chord. Similarly, if the melodic minor form of a scale is used in music, it requires some accidentals. Illustration 19 is taken from the last movement of Haydn's String Quartet Op. 76 No. 3, the famous "Emperor" Quartet. Notice how the cello's part is written largely in the C melodic minor scale. Incidentally, the second chord is a *polychord*—a diminished seventh chord based on B-natural and superimposed on an F-minor chord sketched by the cello. We will talk about poly-chords in a later chapter.

ILLUSTRATION 19

Once you have studied augmented and diminished intervals and altered chords, complete Exercise C on Worksheet #11 and have your teacher check your work.

# WORKSHEET #11

## Exercise A

On the blanks below the intervals, identify each as a second, third, fourth, etc. Also identify each as perfect (P), major (M), minor (m), augmented (A), or diminished (d).

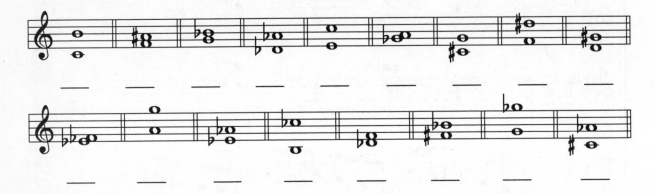

## Exercise B

Write the appropriate chord letter names in the following exercise; be careful with altered chords.

## Exercise C

The following excerpt is taken from the second movement of Haydn's String Quartet Op. 3, No. 5. Write the letter names of the chords on the blanks provided, including sevenths and inversions where appropriate. **Note:** There are several passing tones in the 1st Violin part, including the three C's. Study how Haydn achieves the change of mode in the 1st Violin part.

## Chapter Eleven

# Secondary Dominants, Modulation

In Chapter 10, we discussed altering chords for various reasons. The most common type of altered chord is the secondary dominant. To understand this type of chord, we must review some of the concepts discussed earlier in this book.

## Dominant Chords

In Chapter 2, each step of the scale was given a special name, which suggested its function in the scale. These are listed below:

| Scale step | Name | Note in the C major scale |
|:---:|:---:|:---:|
| 8 | tonic | C |
| 7 | leading tone | B |
| 6 | submediant | A |
| 5 | dominant | G |
| 4 | subdominant | F |
| 3 | mediant | E |
| 2 | supertonic | D |
| 1 | tonic | C |

ILLUSTRATION 1

The dominant note is always a fifth above the *lower* tonic note. When chords are constructed on these scale steps, they take the name of the step. Thus, we speak of a "tonic chord" (a chord that has the tonic note for its root), a "subdominant chord," a "dominant chord," and so on. These relationships remain constant regardless of the key of the work, as may be seen in Illustration 2. The subdominant chord is *always* based on the note a perfect fourth above the tonic, no matter what the key.

A change from one chord to a different chord is called a *chord progression*. Chord progressions are described by the root tones of the chords, regardless of whether the chords involved are in root or in inverted position. In a progression down

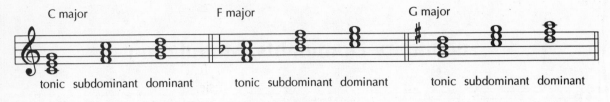

ILLUSTRATION 2

a fifth (as from the dominant to the tonic chord), for example, none of the four voices of the chord may actually move downward a fifth, but we still call it a downward progression of a fifth because that describes the relationship of the two chords' roots.

The strongest progression in any key is the one from the dominant to the tonic chord. Why is this so? For one thing, this progression ends on the tonic, or home tone, chord, giving a strong feeling of finality. For another, the V chord's leading tone is its middle note; you expect that note to move, or resolve, to the tonic note. When the seventh is added to the V chord, there is an even more powerful thrust to the tonic. The $V^7$ chord is quite dissonant, partly because the added seventh clashes with the root of the chord. Another clash within the chord is that between the third and the seventh of the chord—B and F in the key of C (Illustration 3A). This is a diminished fifth, a very unstable interval with a strong tendency to "close in" by half steps to a consonant major third (Illustration 3B).

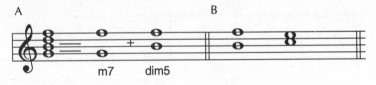

ILLUSTRATIONS 3A and 3B

This tendency of $V^7$ chords to resolve to I chords is so strong that any chord with a major third and a minor seventh sounds like the first part of a $V^7$-to-I progression, and your ear expects to hear I as the next chord. Even in minor keys, as in Illustration 4, the $V^7$ chord is altered to make it major so that the leading tone will be only a half

ILLUSTRATION 4

step from the tonic. Play the progressions in Illustration 5. Which resolution sounds like the "right" (that is, the expected) one?

V⁷    I      V⁷    ♭VI     V⁷    IV⁶

ILLUSTRATION 5

Once you understand dominant chords, do Exercise A on Worksheet #12 and have your teacher check your work.

## Secondary Dominant Chords

Within any given key, the V chord is the main, or *primary*, dominant chord. However, from time to time in a composition, a composer may use a major chord, often with a minor seventh added, that leads to a chord other than the tonic. In effect, the composer is momentarily "borrowing" a dominant-to-tonic progression from *another key*. We have already seen this in Chapter 9 with the song, "America, the Beautiful" (Illustration 8). As described in Chapter 10, the song, which is in C major, briefly borrows from the key of G major. It uses a D⁷ chord leading to a G chord as part of its chord progression. The D⁷, which is the dominant of the G chord, thus becomes a *secondary dominant* chord in that key (the G chord is the primary dominant). In other words, a secondary dominant is a dominant chord of any note but the tonic in a given key. A secondary dominant is symbolized by writing a V or V⁷, a slash, and the number of the chord in the original key to which it resolves. In "America, the Beautiful," it would be symbolized by V⁷/V; the dominant seventh of the V chord in the key of C.

In Illustration 6, there are three chord progressions in three different keys, G, C, and F. In each case, the progression moves from the dominant chord to the tonic within the key. We can use exactly the same progression, but analyze it as being all in one key (F) as in Illustration 7. Notice that all the secondary dominants here are altered chords, and that each of them is the dominant of the chord that follows it. Play this progression over several times to hear how the chords relate.

We have already seen how a secondary dominant chord works in one song. In Illustration 8, we have a simple piano arrangement of the beginning of Stephen Foster's song "My Old Kentucky Home." The first chord is C major, I in the key. The

ILLUSTRATION 6

ILLUSTRATION 7

second chord is also C major, but with an added minor seventh (B-flat). This is a secondary dominant. Since this chord is the dominant seventh in the key of F, we call it $V^7/IV$ (F is the IV chord in the key of C). The first chord in the second full measure is indeed an F chord, but the song returns immediately to the key of C.

ILLUSTRATION 8

Another secondary dominant can be found in Illustration 9. This well-known "Prayer of Thanksgiving" uses harmonies in the key through the first five measures. In measures 6 and 7, however, we have $D^7$ chords. In both cases, these chords resolve to G chords; the $D^7$ chord is the dominant of G. The $D^7$ chords will be marked $V^7/V$ since the G chord is the primary dominant in the key (C).

ILLUSTRATION 9

The V⁷/IV and the V⁷/V are two of the most common secondary dominant chords. Of course, we could leave the seventh out of the V⁷/V and still have a secondary dominant (V/V). As long as a chord is altered to make it dominant, it can be considered a secondary dominant in a major key (in minor keys, as discussed in Chapter Six, primary dominants are also altered chords). However, any chord in a given key may be preceded by a secondary dominant (except, of course, the I chord). Illustration 10 shows all the chords and their secondary dominants in the key of C.

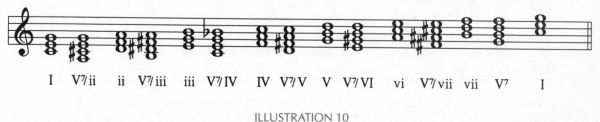

ILLUSTRATION 10

In a different key, of course, a composer must adapt the chords above to fit. For example, let's assume you are writing a V⁷/vi chord in the key of F, which resolves to a vi chord. Begin by determining what the vi chord is in the key of F (d minor); then precede the vi chord by its own dominant seventh chord (A⁷), as in Illustration 11A. If you want to write a V⁷/V in the key of A, begin by determining the V in the key of A (E), and then precede it by its dominant seventh (B⁷), as in Illustration 11B.

ILLUSTRATIONS 11A and 11B

As with all chords, secondary dominants may be written in inverted positions. By inverting the chords in the two examples above, we can improve the voice leading quite a bit (Illustrations 12A and 12B).

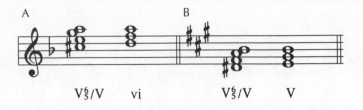

$$V^6_5/V \quad vi \qquad\qquad V^6_5/V \quad V$$

ILLUSTRATIONS 12A and 12B

Once you feel you have mastered the concept of secondary dominants, work Exercise B on Worksheet #12 and have your work checked.

## Chains of Chords

So far we have dealt with secondary dominants resolving to their target triads before going on. There are a lot of songs, however, in which secondary dominants are linked together without intervening chords of resolution. A popular song from the 1920's, "JaDa," excerpted in Illustration 13, makes use of such a chain of secondary dominants. The basic key is G, and the chord in the first measure is G. However, in the second measure the chord is $E^7$—major, not minor. $E^7$ is the dominant of the a chord (ii in G), which is minor. However, the first chord in the third measure is $A^7$, which is the dominant of D (V in G). The $A^7$ chord leads to a $D^7$ ($V^7$), which in turn resolves back to a G chord. The progression here is I-$V^7$/ii-$V^7$/V-$V^7$-I.

$$G\ (I) \qquad E^7\ (V^7/ii) \qquad A^7\ (V^7/V) \qquad D^7\ (V^7) \qquad G\ (I)$$

ILLUSTRATION 13

Another song from the same period, "Five Foot Two, Eyes of Blue," is shown in Illustration 14. This uses an even more elaborate chain of secondary dominants. Beginning with a I chord, its progression is I-$V^7$/vi-$V^7$/ii-$V^7$/V-$V^7$-I.

Secondary dominant chords add an enormous range of flexibility and harmonic color to your technique as an arranger or composer. The principles of good voice leading must still be observed carefully, but you now have the technique to arrange material you couldn't handle before, or to smooth out rough spots in your harmonizations. You can also understand those harmonizations by others that undoubtedly made no sense before. For a final example in this section, the song "Tell Me Why" is given in

ILLUSTRATION 14

Illustration 15, together with its harmonization. Notice the chain of secondary dominants in the fourth phrase.

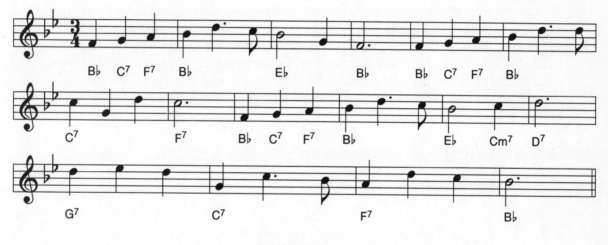

ILLUSTRATION 15

When you have studied this carefully, do Exercise C on Worksheet #12, and have your work checked.

# Modulation

Staying in one basic key is satisfactory for short works (under two or three minutes in length) because the piece ends before its audience can tire of the sound of the key. For longer works, however, especially for pieces that are made up of shorter connected sections (such as the overture to a musical show), moving from one key to another frequently helps avoid the tiresome sameness of hearing one key center for five or more minutes. The importance of making good, smooth-sounding key changes, or *modulations*, can hardly be overstressed.

Consider, for a moment, the philosophy of modulation. The trick is to dissolve the sound of the first key without totally destroying it in one wild jump, and to establish the sound of the new key in some logical way. One *could* simply play a B-flat chord on the piano, sit on the keys, and then play any other chord—a B chord, for example. Try this, and see what the effect is. This would be a modulation of sorts, but not a very subtle one. The sense of flow, which is so important in music, is maintained much more effectively if a smooth link exists between keys. Well-written music is a bit like a conversation: It best moves forward when new subjects flow out of previous comments. Poorly written music is something like a conversation that occurs after an awkward silence when no one can think of anything to say.

Dissolving the first tonality can be done in a number of ways, but most methods involve temporarily increasing the degree of dissonance of the chords and then establishing a new consonance. The easiest modulations to make are those involving changes up or down a fourth. These keys are closely related to the original key since the tonic chords of the new key are important chords in the original key as well. For example, if the original key is B-flat, the key a perfect fourth up is E-flat, and the I chord in E-flat is the IV chord in the original key. Since the IV chord is frequently used, this change of key is easy and natural. Similarly, the key a perfect fourth lower than B-flat is F, whose I chord is the V chord of the original key. This is also an easy and natural change. These keys, as can be seen in Illustrations 16A and 16B, are closely related to the original key.

ILLUSTRATIONS 16A and 16B

## Modulation by Secondary Dominant

At its simplest, a modulation involves a three-chord progression: the last chord in the original key; a *pivot chord* which connects the two keys smoothly; and a chord, often the tonic, in the new key. In Illustration 17A, the B-flat and E-flat chords are the tonics in the two keys. The B-flat seventh chord is the pivot chord. The progression is smooth because the B-flat seventh chord merely adds a minor seventh to the B-flat chord, and this is the dominant of the new key, E-flat.

In Illustration 17B, the B-flat and F chords are the tonics, and the C with a minor seventh is the pivot chord. The C chord is the ii chord in B-flat. Since it must serve as the dominant chord in the new key, however, and since dominant chords are always major, the C chord is made major by raising its third (e-flat) to e-natural.

I    V⁷/IV    IV        I    V⁷/V    V

ILLUSTRATIONS 17A and 17B

In short, this modulation is made through a secondary dominant. In this instance, the key change will continue for some time, usually thirty-two measures at least. When a key change is made, the pivot chord is usually accounted for in both the old and the new keys. Thus, a B-flat to E-flat modulation would be indicated as in Illustration 18A; a B-flat to F modulation would be indicated as in Illustration 18B.

Bb: I    V⁷/IV            Bb: I    V⁷/V
Eb:      V⁷        I      F:       V⁷        I

ILLUSTRATIONS 18A and 18B

The principle of modulation by secondary dominant can be extended to all the secondary dominant chords within a given key. If we wish to modulate from the key of B-flat to the key of G major, for example, we may do so smoothly as is shown in Illustration 19. Since G, the tonic of the new key, is already the sixth step of the B-flat scale, we can modulate through the dominant chord of the vi chord. If the D⁷ chord were not used for modulation, but merely as a secondary dominant within the key of B-flat, the G chord to which the pivot chord resolves would be minor, since the g-minor chord is the vi chord in B-flat major. In a modulation, however, it doesn't matter whether the new key is in minor or major mode. Obviously, G major (one sharp) is more distantly related to B-flat major (two flats) than is g minor (also two flats). Nonetheless, the transition from B-flat to G is an easy one to accomplish by means of a secondary dominant.

Bb:  I      V⁷/vi

G:       V⁷        I

ILLUSTRATION 19

Let's examine another secondary dominant modulation before moving on. Such modulations can be made from the original key to any key that is represented in *either the major or minor mode* of the original key. Assume that you have a section of a piece in the key of E major, and you want to change it to d minor. The note D-natural does not exist in the major scale of E, but it is found in the scale of e minor. Even though we begin the modulation in Illustration 20 in E major, we can smoothly go to d minor with one secondary dominant pivot chord, $A^7$.

E:  I      V⁷/vii

d:       V⁷        i

ILLUSTRATION 20

## *Modulation by Diminished Seventh Chord*

Modulations using a secondary dominant chord as a pivot are one means of increasing the dissonance in order to establish a new tonal center. A second method is to use the diminished seventh chord. A diminished seventh chord, you will recall, is a diminished triad with a diminished (that is, doubly lowered) seventh added. The term diminished seventh is admittedly a bit confusing; to be more precise, we should say, "a diminished triad with a diminished seventh added." Say that mouthful several times and you will appreciate why the shorter form is commonly used.

The diminished seventh chord consists of notes a minor third apart from their nearest adjacent notes. Since it belongs to no key, it makes an ideal pivot chord. In practical terms, there are only three possible diminished seventh chords, as shown in Illustration 21. All others are simply restructurings of one of the basic three. The

ILLUSTRATION 21

diminished seventh based on D, for example, uses the same pitches as the one based on B, except that the note B is called by its enharmonic equivalent, C-flat, in the D chord.

The diminished seventh is such a versatile pivot chord because *each of its notes may be used either as the leading tone or as the tonic of a new key*. In Illustration 22, each progression starts from the same two chords, leading to the same pitches (with enharmonic spellings), and resolving to four different keys, depending on which note of the diminished seventh chord is chosen to be the leading tone. In each case, the leading tone is in the bass voice.

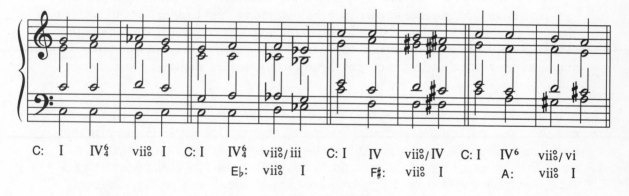

ILLUSTRATION 22

In Illustration 23, we have the same two chords at the beginning of the progression, but this time each of the pitches of the diminished seventh is taken as the tonic of the new key. In each case, the final tonic is in the soprano voice.

Therefore we can make eight modulations using the same pivot chord in different ways. Keep in mind that any of these forms of the diminished seventh chord can resolve to either the major or the minor mode of the new key. Therefore, the three diminished seventh chords allow forty-eight possible resolutions (twenty-four each to major or minor keys) in three easy steps.

ILLUSTRATION 23

This kind of all-purpose solution does have its problems. The biggest is that the diminished seventh chord is a powerful "key solvent." It has been nicknamed the "chord of chaos" because it destroys a tonality and leaves the listener in a state of total ambiguity—one has no idea what will follow. For most modulations, you don't want such a total obliteration of key; one doesn't swat flies with a wrecking ball. If you're changing to an easy key, say, from C to F or G, there is no need to go through such a potent pivot chord. Other, less radical solutions are available.

The diminished seventh chord also has a very distinctive, characteristic sound. If overused, it will become trite and irritating. The listener is apt to adopt an attitude of "here he goes again with his modulation-by-diminished-seventh bit." You can use this chord once or twice as a modulation chord in a fairly lengthy work, but using the diminished seventh chord more often will very likely weaken the total effect of your work.

Sometimes one can prolong the time period of the modulation itself. This can make the total effect more interesting. Suppose you are in the key of G and wish to modulate to a remote key, such as D-flat. The most direct way to do so is through a C diminished-seventh chord. In the second chord in Illustration 24, G-flat is written enharmonically as F-sharp to take advantage of the original key signature. This may

ILLUSTRATION 24

seem rather abrupt, but the process can be lengthened in a number of ways. One method is to introduce chords with more flats in them (since we are going to a key in flats) between the two tonic chords. The starting key, G, has one sharp; the final key, D-flat, has five flats in its signature. We can introduce some of these flats early by changing to g minor, which needs no preparation, before getting to the diminished seventh chord, as in Illustration 25.

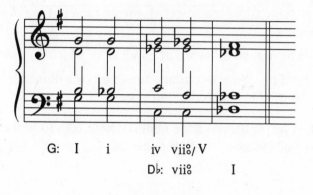

ILLUSTRATION 25

## Modulation by Melodic Sequence

Still another method of modulation is to use a *melodic sequence* that moves through a number of different keys. A string of dominant pivot chords usually provides the dissolving effect in sequence modulations, as in Illustration 26. In this

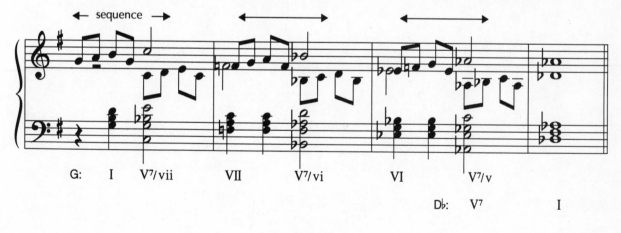

ILLUSTRATION 26

illustration, the melody (treble staff, stems upward) is repeated three times, each successive time a whole step lower; this process is called a melodic sequence. The bass moves by perfect fifths and fourths, making a strong, lively root progression. The second chord in each measure is a dominant pivot chord in a new key and resolves to its new tonic. The minor seventh added to each pivot chord provides the necessary dissonance to dissolve the previous key feeling, yet the changes in key are smooth and flowing. Here is yet another way to get from the key of G to the key of D-flat.

This section has introduced you to a few of the standard ways of modulating, or changing key. It is by no means an exhaustive list of ways, and we will discover still others later in the book. The main points to keep in mind are the following:

1.  You may need to change the key center from time to time in your compositions or arrangements.

2.  To do so, you have several means at hand, all of which involve a pivot chord.

3.  The pivot chord may be a secondary dominant or a diminished seventh chord. Either may be used in a melodic sequence.

Once you feel you understand the material here, turn to Worksheet #12 and work Exercise D. Have your teacher check the results.

## Exercise A

In each measure below, the chord given is the tonic of a key. Write the dominant seventh chord in root position in the space following the chord.

## Exercise B

Write the indicated chords on the bass staff. Mark asterisks (*) over all secondary dominants.

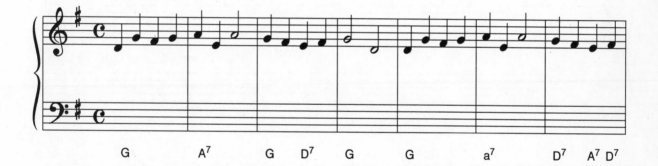

G  A⁷  G D⁷ G  G  a⁷  D⁷ A⁷ D⁷

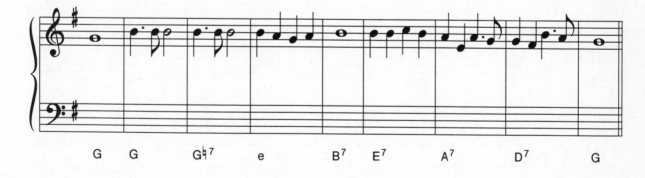

G G G♮⁷  e   B⁷ E⁷  A⁷  D⁷  G

## Exercise C

Beneath the chords, write the numbers that describe the progression.

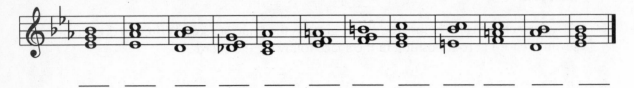

_____  _____  _____  _____  _____  _____  _____  _____  _____  _____

## Exercise D

A. Complete a modulation progression from the indicated chord to the key of A, using a secondary dominant as a pivot chord.

B. Complete a modulation progression from the indicated chord to the key of D flat, using a diminished seventh as a pivot chord.

C. Modulate by melodic sequence from the first measure to the key of B major.

A

B

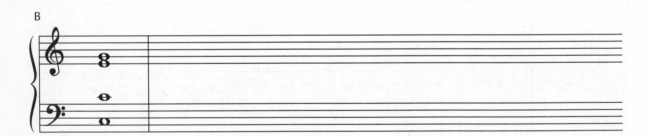

C

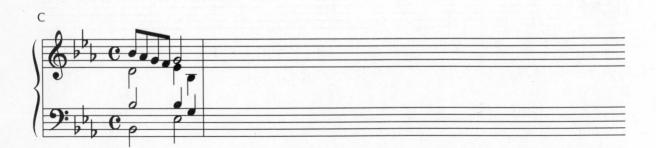

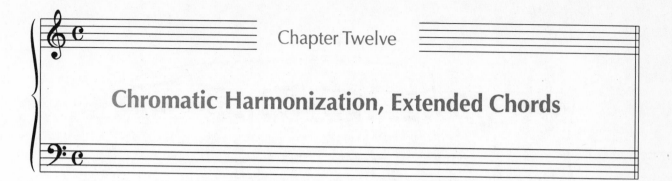

# Chromatic Harmonization, Extended Chords

## Chromatic Harmonization

Up to now, our attention has been focused almost entirely on harmonizing music written in diatonic (that is, major or minor) scales. Harmonizing chromatic music requires some techniques of chord writing that you have only recently learned. In this section, we'll explore some of the standard ways chromatic passages have been harmonized by experts in the craft.

Before we get going, let's think about why we might use chromatic effects. Music is an expression of feelings that can induce emotions in the listener. Composers must therefore be aware of what sorts of feelings they want to create in listeners. In our culture, we associate major key music with many moods—happiness, calm, joyful excitement, brightness, security, and so on. These various moods are influenced by the particular chords used, the instrumentation, the speed or loudness chosen, and many other factors. As a general rule, "major equals happy" is an accurate statement.

Minor key music, on the other hand, usually creates an atmosphere of either sadness or menace. We associate minor keys with sorrow, peril, comic grotesqueness, despair, doom, or fright, again depending on harmony, speed, loudness, and instrumentation.

Chromatic effects are used for certain other moods, such as sustained tension, instability or uncertainty, grief, or impending danger. The sound of wind blowing is frequently imitated by chromatic-scale passages, as in Illustration 1. Something falling or descending is often depicted by a descending chromatic scale, as in Illustration 2.

Chromatic scales can also depict drooping spirits. Sadness and grief are often characterized in this way. One of the most affecting portrayals of sorrow in all musical literature is the aria known as "Dido's Lament" from Henry Purcell's opera *Dido and Aeneas.* Dido's melody is largely diatonic (minor key), but it is set over a repeated bass figure (Illustration 3) which is largely chromatic. Listen to this work, and notice how the constantly descending bass gives a feeling of profound sorrow to the aria.

In his tone poem "Les Préludes," Franz Liszt frequently used chromatic scales to create feelings of tension and excitement. In the passage given in Illustration 4, he

ILLUSTRATION 1

ILLUSTRATION 2

ILLUSTRATION 3

builds up tremendous tension with this musical idea. In another part of the same piece he whirls the listener around in a veritable cyclone of sound, as seen in Illustration 5.

ILLUSTRATION 4

Chromatic scales can also be used to suggest an exotic, often Oriental, setting. One example of this may be found in Claude Debussy's solo for unaccompanied flute entitled "Syrinx." The chromatic melody (Illustration 6) suggests a mythological satyr noodling on his panpipes.

These are some of the *effects* of chromatic passages. Now let's turn our attention to harmonizing some of these effects. The simplest type of chromatic harmonization is to treat the chromatically changed note as an alteration of the "intended" note. This is

ILLUSTRATION 5

ILLUSTRATION 6

most successful when it occurs on a weak beat of the measure, as in Illustration 7. In this illustration, the flute's G-sharp sounds like an augmented fifth of the chord; it gets its meaning as a passing tone between the fifth and sixth scale steps (all parts in concert pitch).

ILLUSTRATION 7

In Illustration 8, the flute's F-sharp and G-sharp are really just melodic embellishments; they do not affect the harmony in any way. Sometimes, as in Illustration 9,

ILLUSTRATION 8

chromatic notes simply represent changes in a chord's mode, from minor to major or vice versa.

ILLUSTRATION 9

Another type of chromatic harmonization occurs when two voices move in parallel chromatic lines, usually thirds or sixths. Study Illustration 10 carefully. At the beginning of each measure is a strong chord in the original key. These chords provide the stability of a key center, even though the melody and harmony are quite chromatic. In a given piece, chords on the strong beats determine how strong the feeling of key center will be.

ILLUSTRATION 10

Still another approach to harmonization of chromatic lines is shown in Illustration 11. Each altered (raised or lowered) note is harmonized by a secondary dominant chord. Because no fewer than three of the four voices change pitch in each chord, this is a rather cumbersome harmonization technique. It sounds best when the chord changes are relatively slow, in eighth notes or longer. When rapid parts are harmonized this way, the result is apt to sound thick and muddy.

ILLUSTRATION 11

Chromatic lines may also be treated as successions of passing tones. Care must be taken, though, that the melodic notes are in chords at the strongest rhythmic points—on each beat, or on beats 1 and 3 in common time, as in Illustration 12. The chromatic notes fill in between strong chord tones with exciting results. Notice that in Illustration 12B, the I chord is major but the iv chord is minor in order to harmonize the D-flat in the melody.

ILLUSTRATIONS 12A and 12B

It should be obvious that chromatic melodies tend to weaken the sense of key center just as diatonic melodies reinforce the feeling of home tone. Illustration 13 shows one simple and nifty way to change from one key to a distantly related key; simply place an unharmonized, unison chromatic passage between them. In effect, the unison chromatic scale "dissolves" the original key (F). A new key may be established almost anywhere by simply playing a new tonic chord.

ILLUSTRATION 13

Feelings of uncertainty, instability, and even menace can thus be evoked by using chromatic sections. For the ultimate in such "non-key" effects, parallel diminished seventh chords can suggest impending disaster, as in Illustration 14.

ILLUSTRATION 14

Once you feel you have mastered this section, you should work Exercise A of Worksheet #13. As always, have your teacher check your work.

## Ninth Chords

By now you should be quite comfortable dealing with triads and seventh chords. With what you have learned so far, you can analyze, arrange, or write music in the styles of a large percentage of the compositions you hear or perform. Much concert music, as well as popular idioms like country and western or folk music, seldom venture far beyond the harmonic technique you already understand. Most rock music, too, uses simple chord forms, although the progressions may be rather different.

One of the fascinations of musical theory, however, is that there is always more to learn and to master. To illustrate this point, play the chord in Illustration 15. How

ILLUSTRATION 15

would you analyze this chord? It contains an F triad, obviously; add the E-flat and you have an $F^7$ chord. But how can we explain the G? Looked at in another way, it might appear to be a C-minor triad (CE-flatG) placed on top of an F-major triad; in short, a polychord. Later on, we'll study polychords in more depth. But the simplest answer for the moment is to call our chord an *F ninth chord*.

Our coverage of harmony has involved the study of triads at an early stage. Then we learned that, in order to create seventh chords, we add a new note a third above the top note of a triad. The term *seventh chord* indicates that a new note a seventh above the root of the chord is added. To make a ninth chord, you simply continue the process of piling thirds on the top for one more step, as in Illustration 15. The new note is a ninth above the root. It might seem more logical to term this a *second* chord because the new note is a second and an octave above the root. Such a chord appears in Illustration 16A; notice that the texture is much thicker than the arrangement of pitches in the ninth chord. In practice, you should usually keep a distance of at least a ninth between the root and the added ninth, as in Illustration 16B, no matter what inversion the chord is in.

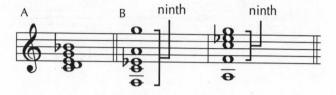

ILLUSTRATIONS 16A and 16B

Ninth chords in traditional harmony, such as we have been studying so far, are used very rarely as a special "color" chord. Usually, a ninth chord appears as a $V_7^9$ in some key, or as a secondary dominant, as in Illustration 17. When inverted, it is always written in one of the three inversions already discussed—$V_5^6$, $V_3^4$, or $V^2$—with an added ninth. The ninth is never found in the bass, except perhaps as a quick passing tone.

If you are writing for four parts, whether instruments or voices, you obviously can't have all five notes of the ninth chord represented. The usual solution is to omit the fifth of the chord (in its root position), and to include the root, third, seventh, and ninth, as in Illustration 17.

ILLUSTRATION 17

Ninths often appear as held-over, or *suspended*, notes from a previous chord. They then resolve to a different chord tone while the other parts stay still, as in Illustration 18. Notice that the soprano's A first appears in the IV chord, then carries over while the other parts move to a $V^7$ chord. The A then drops to G, while the other parts stay on their notes. The suspended ninth adds a spicy extra dissonance to the $V^7$ chord.

Ninths, like the seconds they closely resemble, come in major, minor, augmented, and (seldom) diminished forms. A major ninth sounds slightly less dissonant than a minor ninth, as can be heard in Illustration 19A. The minor ninth often gives a very interesting color to a chord when it is not the highest note, as in Illustration 19B. The augmented ninth is a rather rare specimen. It is usually replaced by its near-identical twin, the minor tenth (Illustration 20). In jazz composition and arranging, ending a piece on an augmented ninth chord can produce a pungent, dissonant effect. We will come back to this idea in a later chapter.

ILLUSTRATION 18

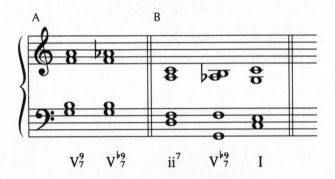

ILLUSTRATIONS 19A and 19B

ILLUSTRATION 20

## Other Extended Chords

Ninths are one type of extended chord; there are many others—tenths, elevenths, twelfths, thirteenths, and fourteenths. Remember that tenths and twelfths duplicate intervals in the basic triad: the tenth is an octave above the third, the twelfth is an octave above the fifth. If these notes simply duplicate the lower pitch, they are not described as tenths and twelfths, but merely as octaves of the lower pitch. Only when the tenth is a different pitch from the third, or the twelfth is a different pitch from the fifth (i.e., a minor tenth with a major third, or an augmented twelfth with a perfect fifth) do we use the term *tenth* or *twelfth*. A fifteenth would simply be an octave doubling of the tonic, a virtually useless interval; chords extended beyond the four-teenth are better described in some other way, such as tone clusters.

Tenths could theoretically come in major, minor, augmented, and diminished forms; three of these intervals are best used in other ways. A major tenth simply doubles a major third an octave higher; an augmented tenth is better written as a perfect eleventh; and a diminished tenth sounds like a major ninth. In practical terms, therefore, the minor tenth is the common form of tenth used. This is because when it's added to a major chord, as in Illustration 21A, it adds an edgy, "bluesy" flavor. One could also add a major tenth to a minor chord (Illustration 21B). Unless used carefully (and sparingly), this form sounds as though one of the performers played a wrong note.

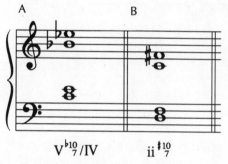

ILLUSTRATIONS 21A and 21B

Elevenths and twelfths, like fourths and fifths, come in perfect, augmented, and diminished forms. Perfect elevenths are quite dissonant and are seldom used in four-part writing because they clash strongly with the third of the chord, as in Illustration 22A. Chords with a perfect eleventh usually have more than four voices to them, as in jazz arranging; the extra tones soften the dissonance of the interval (Illustration 22B). Augmented elevenths (or their twins, diminished twelfths) are very useful and color-ful chords. Once more, they work best in thick-textured, five- or six-voiced chords. Their spicy "bite" is a popular sound in jazz (Illustration 22C).

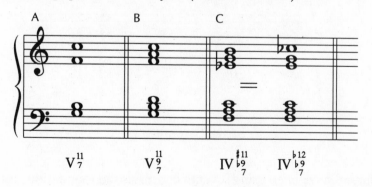

ILLUSTRATIONS 22A, 22B, and 22C

The diminished twelfth is the twin of the augmented eleventh, of course, and the perfect twelfth duplicates the fifth of the original chord, so it is seldom used. Thirteenths, like sixths, come in two main forms, major and minor. They normally appear in chords with five or more voices, and are useful for adding a dissonant, close-textured quality to the chord. The dominant chord with a major thirteenth, a minor ninth, and a minor seventh makes a lovely, rich chord (Illustration 23A). The fourteenth chord is rarely used, except where the chord has a major seventh and a minor fourteenth, or vice versa. Here again, a very dense chord with five or more voices is called for. Two versions of fourteenth chords appear in Illustration 23B.

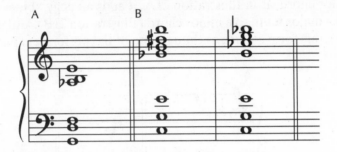

ILLUSTRATIONS 23A and 23B

With so much material to choose from, it is quite possible to have all seven scale degrees in one chord, perhaps with certain notes modified by raising or lowering. Examine the chords in Illustration 24. Each contains all the notes of the scale, some of them flatted or sharped. Play the chords on the piano (a trick that will require two players!) and listen to the effect each achieves. Below each chord is the chord symbol for that chord; this is how such chords are written in sheet music. You won't often come across a chord with all seven pitches.

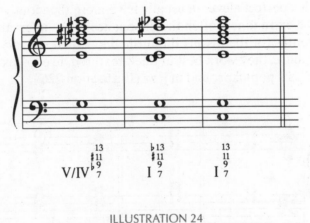

ILLUSTRATION 24

Thus far, we have been using seventh chords as the foundations for extended chords. Another type of four-pitch chord often combines well with other extended notes. This chord is the triad with an added major sixth, as seen in Illustration 25A.

This chord is less dissonant than a seventh chord but sounds fuller and richer than a simple triad. When a major sixth is added to a triad, you need to include the entire triad; otherwise, the chord sounds like a vi chord in first inversion, as in Illustration 25B. To indicate a triad with an added sixth, rather than a first inversion, write "+6" after the Roman numeral. Major ninths sound lush and stable when combined with chords with added sixths, as in Illustration 25C.

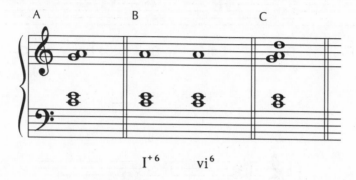

ILLUSTRATIONS 25A, 25B, and 25C

Of the chords introduced in this chapter, only the ninth and the added sixth chords can be used readily in four-part writing. When adding more dissonance with the higher notes of the chord, it becomes increasingly important to have a solid, basic triad at the bottom of the chord. Otherwise, the chord ceases to sound like that chord in that key, and begins to sound like a "wrong" chord borrowed from another key. The more tones added to a chord (ninths, elevenths, and so on), the more dissonant it becomes, and the more necessary the basic triad becomes to defining the chord relative to other chords in the key. This often requires more than four voices to accomplish.

Complex, dissonant chords are usually used in compositions or arrangements where *all* the chords are of similar dissonance. In such pieces a curious thing occurs: Chords of moderate or great dissonance need not strictly follow the principles of voice leading or progressions by fourths and fifths that are necessary with less dissonant pieces. In fact, you can even use chords from entirely unrelated keys and the piece will sound "right." Play the chords in Illustration 26; notice the names of the chords written below each one.

When writing out the chord symbols of extended chords using Roman and Arabic numerals, it is customary to indicate the basic chord's inversion in the usual way, and then to show which *other* notes have been added. For example, if a $V^7$ chord in second inversion has an added ninth, the chord is indicated as $V^9_{\substack{4\\3}}$, regardless of how far above the bass the ninth actually appears (Illustration 27A). Similarly, a $IV^7$ chord in first inversion with an added minor ninth and augmented eleventh will be indicated as shown in Illustration 27B. Keep in mind that the ninth will usually be *at least* a ninth above the root; otherwise, the chord will resemble a tone cluster, a form of chord we will study in a later chapter.

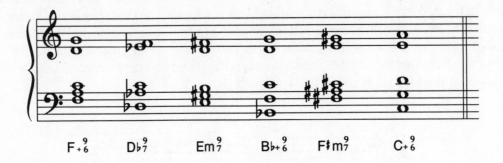

$$F_{+6}^{9} \quad Db_{7}^{9} \quad Em_{7}^{9} \quad Bb_{+6}^{9} \quad F\sharp m_{7}^{9} \quad C_{+6}^{9}$$

ILLUSTRATION 26

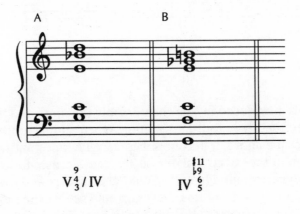

$$V_{3}^{9}{}_{4}/IV \qquad IV_{5}^{\sharp 11}{}_{\flat 9}{}_{6}$$

ILLUSTRATIONS 27A and 27B

Once you feel you understand extended chords, complete Exercise B on Worksheet #13, and have your teacher check your work.

## Exercise A

1. Harmonize the following melody, using one chord per measure.

2. Use a chromatic unison to change key in this exercise from B-flat to B.

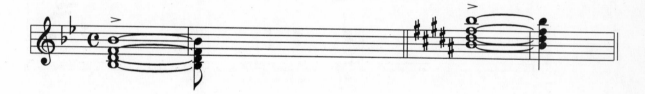

## Exercise B

1. Write out each of the chords indicated below, using only four notes for each.

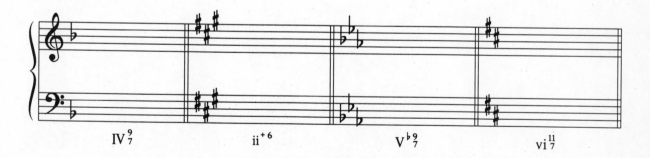

$$\text{IV}_7^9 \qquad \text{ii}^{+6} \qquad \text{V}_7^{\flat 9} \qquad \text{vi}_7^{11}$$

2. The following excerpt is taken from Debussy's "Prelude to the Afternoon of a Faun." Below each chord write its letter, its inversion, and any extensions. **Note**: This piece uses very nontraditional harmonies. In places there are single basic chords with chromatic modifications of certain notes. In other places, there are

pedal notes with other chords written above the pedals. Analyze as many chords as you can.

# Altered Sixth Chords, Nonharmonic Tones

The majority of chords used in any composition or arrangement are chords of the basic key; accidentals are the exception, not the rule. Even chromatic passages are usually brief and appear as either special effects or a means of modulation from one key to another. But there are a number of special "color" chords that can be used to add interest to an otherwise bland harmonization. Think of them as salt for your harmonic mashed potatoes. These special chords are also useful for changing key.

The four chords described in this section are examples of such color chords. All of them are first-inversion chords, or *sixth chords*, in which certain notes are altered by accidentals. They are also given names implying a foreign origin, although there is no basis in fact for this implication; as with everything in music, they are quite international in character. The four chords are called the Neapolitan sixth, the Italian sixth, the German sixth, and the French sixth.

## Neapolitan Sixth Chords

The term Neapolitan, applied to sixths or to ice cream, means "from Naples" (Italy). No one knows why this chord has this name. It is usually a first-inversion chord, although sometimes it is used in root position, and it is based on the lowered second degree of a scale, as in Illustration 1. In a chord progression, it usually func-

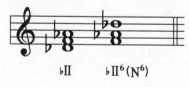

ILLUSTRATION 1

tions as a modified IV chord, because in its inverted state it has the subdominant note (4) in the bass, as in Illustrations 2A and 2B. The Neapolitan sixth ($N^6$) chord may lead to the V chord, as in Illustration 2A, or to the $I_4^6$ followed by the V, as in Illustration 2B.

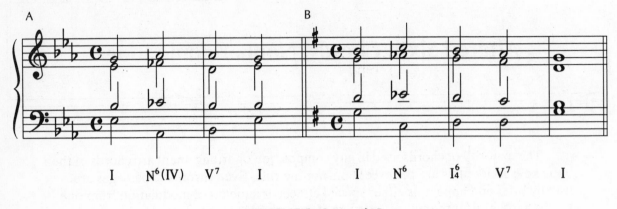

ILLUSTRATIONS 2A and 2B

In another common chord progression, the N$^6$ leads to a diminished seventh chord, as in Illustration 3.

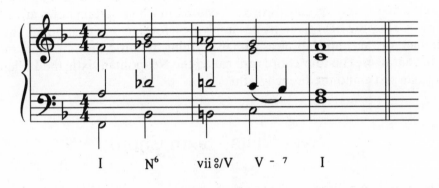

ILLUSTRATION 3

Neapolitan sixth chords are frequently used in minor mode, as in Illustration 4, although they work nicely in either mode.

ILLUSTRATION 4

The bass note (in first inversion) should not be doubled, of course, as with any first-inversion chord, and all the rules of normal voice leading should be observed. In a progression N$^6$-V (Illustration 5), it may be useful to use a V$^7$ chord and to leave out its fifth. Otherwise, you get a clash (called a *cross relation*) between a lowered pitch in one chord and the natural note in the following chord. Such clashes should be avoided in all chord progressions, especially if the work is to be sung, since the altered pitch may throw off the singer of the unaltered pitch which follows.

ILLUSTRATION 5

As with any altered chord, the $N^6$ may be used as the pivot chord of a modulation. Since it is a major triad, it can be used in place of many other major chords in a new key—as a dominant, as a subdominant, as a secondary dominant, or as a new tonic. Illustration 6 shows four ways in which an $N^6$ chord may be used as the pivot chord of a modulation.

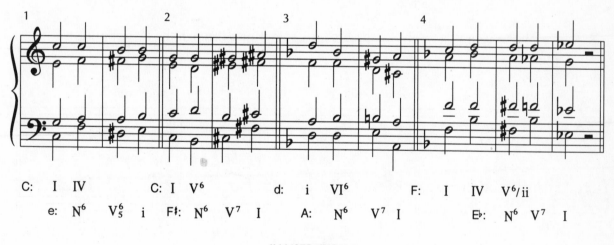

ILLUSTRATION 6

# Augmented Sixth Chords

Neapolitan sixth chords have a minor sixth between the bass (in first inversion) and the root of the chord. By contrast, all the augmented sixth chords have an augmented sixth between bass and root. Augmented sixth chords get their interesting character from the fact that they *sound* like dominant seventh chords, as in Illustration 7A, but they *resolve* quite differently, as in Illustration 7B. It is easiest to think of augmented sixth chords as IV chords in first inversion, with the root raised a half step and the bass lowered a half step, as in Illustration 7C.

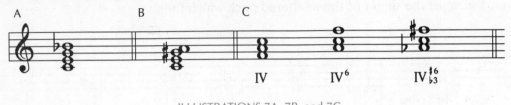

ILLUSTRATIONS 7A, 7B, and 7C

The simplest of the augmented sixth chords is the Italian sixth, which has only three pitches (Illustration 8A). The German sixth chord is a four-pitch chord, with a minor seventh added above the root of the unaltered chord (Illustration 8B). The French sixth chord also has four pitches, but differs in that it has a major sixth added above the root in the basic position, rather than a minor seventh (Illustration 8C).

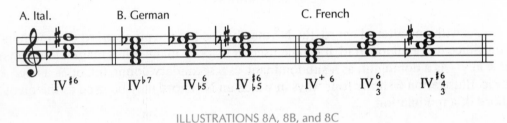

ILLUSTRATIONS 8A, 8B, and 8C

All three chords resolve to the V chord, sometimes through the I$_4^6$, as in Illustration 9.

ILLUSTRATION 9

Study Illustration 10 to see how such a chord might be used in an actual composition. Can you identify the form of the augmented sixth chord used in this illustration? Notice how in the second measure the soprano and bass move chromatically in opposite directions to an octave; this makes a very strong progression. Notice also that the series of chords based on the I$_4^6$ chord does not change the sound of the I$_4^6$ chord; no actual harmonic change takes place. This leads smoothly to the V$^7$ chord in the fourth

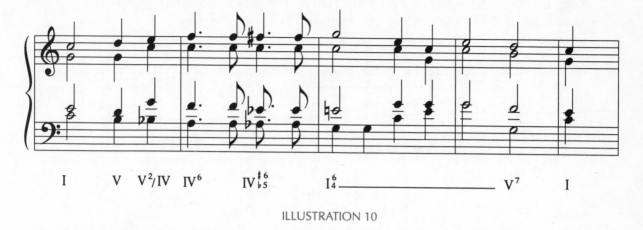

ILLUSTRATION 10

measure. The six beats analyzed as $I_4^6$ need not be described as $I_4^6, I, I^6, I_4^6$ because there is no harmonic change throughout this section.

When you feel confident that you understand the Neapolitan sixth and the augmented sixth chords, complete Exercise A on Worksheet #14, and have your teacher check your work.

## Modulation

Augmented sixth chords make valuable color chords available to the composer or arranger. Because they sound so much like dominant seventh chords, they can also be used to make very surprising modulations. Suppose, for instance, that you want to modulate from C major to E major. It can be done by using the secondary dominant of E ($B^7$) and thus to E, as in Illustration 11A; but you can also use an augmented sixth for the pivot chord. Since B is the dominant of E, you can find the augmented sixth chord that would lead to B—the chord based on A-sharp (Illustration 11B).

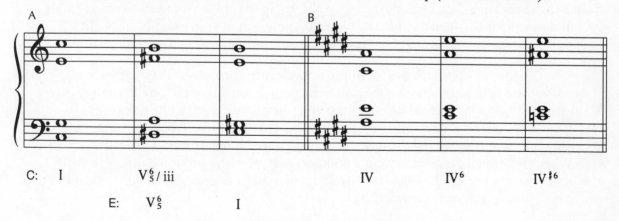

ILLUSTRATIONS 11A and 11B

Since this chord *sounds* like a $C^7$ ($V^7$/IV) chord, it makes a strong but unexpected pivot chord between the two keys (Illustration 12).

C:    I         $V^7$/IV

E:                   IV$^{\sharp 6}_{\flat 5}$        I$^6_4$         $V^7$         I

ILLUSTRATION 12

It should be obvious by now that any chord structured like a dominant seventh chord—that is, with a major third and a minor seventh or augmented sixth above its root—can be used as an augmented sixth chord, and can be resolved in surprising ways. Study the examples of augmented sixth chord modulations in Illustration 13, noting how the pivot chords are used. Each augmented sixth chord is labeled as Italian, German, or French; the labels are not important, but the various types of chords used are worth mastering. Once you fully understand the process of modulating by augmented sixth chord, do Exercise B on Worksheet #14, and have your teacher examine your work.

## Nonharmonic Tones

In our discussion of harmony so far, we have mainly been concerned with placing a chord with every single note of the melody, taking care that the melody notes appear in the supporting chord. In this section, we're going to explore some interesting disagreements between melody and chord that often appear in a composition. In order to begin, we must shift our viewpoint from chordal writing to melodic writing.

Composers approach writing music in two contrasting ways: They write *simultaneous* sounds, or harmony; and they write *successive* sounds, or melody. Harmony is often thought of as vertical writing, since you stack notes in piles, like bricks or Lego™ blocks, as in Illustration 14. Melody is thought of as horizontal writing. The notes are separate like links in a chain, or like Poppet™ beads, as in Illustration 15. When two or more melodies occur simultaneously, or when a round harmonizes with itself, you have to think both vertically and horizontally at once. The result is called *counterpoint*, or *contrapuntal writing*.

In Illustration 16, we see the round called "Three Blind Mice," written out as it would be performed by three singers. The resulting chords are indicated only when

ILLUSTRATION 13

ILLUSTRATION 14

ILLUSTRATION 15

the third voice enters, since before that point there are no three-pitch chords. In most of the measures, every note of the melody fits into the chord. In measures 9, 11, and 13, however, there is one note in the top voice that does not appear in the chord (Illustration 17A). This note derives from the need for a smooth and interesting melody rather than from the harmony. If we substitute a chord tone for this non-chord tone (the A), the result is more conventional harmony, but a much less interesting melody.

ILLUSTRATION 16

Try playing or singing the song, using the measures from Illustration 17B or 17C in place of 17A in measures 9, 11, and 13. Which of these versions do you prefer?

ILLUSTRATIONS 17A, 17B, and 17C

In Illustration 16, the non-chord, or *nonharmonic*, tone is approached from the next higher tone and returns to that tone. The nonharmonic tone is, therefore, the lower neighbor of the chord tone and is called (are you ready for this?) a *lower neighboring tone*. This type of nonharmonic tone appears frequently in various pieces of music. In each of the examples in Illustration 18, the star (★) marks the lower neighboring tone.

ILLUSTRATIONS 18A, 18B, and 18C

Just as there are *lower* neighboring tones, there are also *upper neighboring tones*—nonharmonic tones that are approached scalewise from a lower chord tone, and that return to the same chord tone. In Illustration 19, the notes marked with asterisks are upper neighboring tones.

Another form of nonharmonic tone is the *passing tone*, which appears in scalewise sections of melodies where the preceding and following tones are both chord tones. The asterisks in Illustration 20 mark passing tones.

There are several other types of nonharmonic tones that often appear in music. In Illustration 21, the D in the second measure (tenor voice) is a chord tone on beats 1 and 2. However, on beat 3 the chord changes, and the tenor's D is now a nonharmonic tone. Since it is carried over from a previous chord *in the same voice*, it is called a *suspension*. On beat 3 of the second measure, then, the tenor has a suspended note that moves to a chord tone on beat 4.

Keep in mind that a suspension is nonharmonic in the new chord. The held-over note in Illustration 22 (soprano in measure 2) is not a suspension, because both

A. Ach, Du Lieber Augustin

B. Boston Come-All-Ye

C. Hot Time in the Old Town Tonight

G       G   l.n.   G   l.n.   G

ILLUSTRATIONS 19A, 19B, and 19C

A. Go Tell It on the Mountain

B. Down in the Valley

F       F       G       G       G

C. Springfield Mountain

A       E⁷      E⁷      A

ILLUSTRATIONS 20A, 20B, and 20C

I   IV   I⁶₄   V – ⁷   I

ILLUSTRATION 21

soprano notes are harmonic in the new chord. The soprano's quarter note is simply a delayed chord tone, adding the seventh to the dominant chord.

ILLUSTRATION 22

Just as you can have nonharmonic tones carried over into a later chord, you can also have a nonharmonic tone that starts *before* the chord with which it harmonizes. This type of nonharmonic tone is called an *anticipation.* The anticipations in Illustration 23 are all marked by asterisks; notice that these notes are actually members of the chords that follow their appearance.

ILLUSTRATION 23

The nonharmonic tones examined so far all have two things in common: First, they are all approached and left by scalewise steps; second, they all fall on weak beats in the measure. When a nonharmonic tone appears on a strong beat of the measure, the effect is more of a jolt to the listener because it sounds momentarily like a mistake. This effect is given the name of *appoggiatura* (uh-POJ-yuh-TOUR-ah), which comes from an Italian word meaning "to lean." The appoggiatura leans into a chord tone a scale step away. Tchaikovsky wrote one of the most famous appoggiature in musical history in his overture *Romeo and Juliet.* The "love theme" begins as shown in Illustration 24.

One can get some nice appoggiatura effects with the spiritual "Michael, Row the Boat Ashore" by using a somewhat different harmonization. In Illustration 25, the appoggiature are marked with asterisks; the note marked with a "u.n." is an upper neighboring tone. Try singing this illustration with an autoharp, guitar, or piano accompaniment.

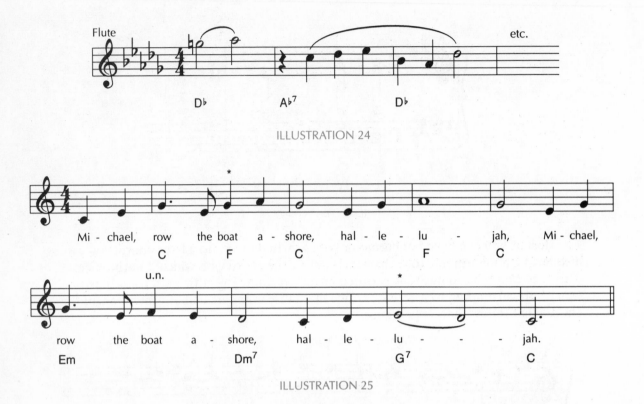

ILLUSTRATION 24

ILLUSTRATION 25

Still another form of nonharmonic tone is the *pedal point*, so called because it can be performed on an organ by holding one foot pedal down. Pedal points usually occur in the bass voice, although they sometimes appear in other voices. Illustration 26 is an example of a pedal point taken from Czech composer Antonin Dvořák's *Symphony No. 9*, subtitled "From the New World." Notice that the dominant pedal point in the first four measures is replaced by a tonic pedal point. The effect in the first four measures is of changing chords, but the pedal point causes the whole passage to sound like some type of dominant chord.

ILLUSTRATION 26

Pedal points can occur on various degrees of the scale, although dominant and tonic are probably most common. In J. S. Bach's well-known *Toccata and Fugue in D Minor*, there is a magnificent, biting dissonance as the pedal anticipates the tonic (D)

while the chord above the pedal is a dominant seventh. Illustration 27 shows the
beginning of the toccata.

ILLUSTRATION 27

The nonharmonic tones we have discussed—anticipations and suspensions,
upper and lower neighboring tones, appoggiature, passing tones, and pedal points—
add greatly to the interest of melodies, and enable you to be much more creative with
your harmonizations.

When you feel you are ready, work Exercise C on Worksheet #14 and have your
teacher check the result.

## Exercise A

1. Write out the indicated chords for the bass line given below. As always, work for the smoothest voice leading you can achieve.

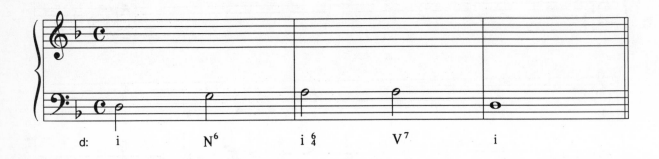

d:   i        N⁶        i ⁶₄        V⁷        i

2. Write out the augmented sixth chords indicated below, using the proper forms of the chords.

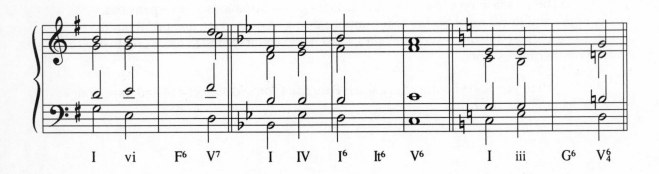

I    vi    F⁶    V⁷    I    IV    I⁶    It⁶    V⁶    I    iii    G⁶    V⁶₄

## Exercise B

Write out the indicated modulations, using the augmented sixth chords as pivot chords.

D:   I   V²   It⁶     F:   I   IV   G⁶     A:   I   IV   vi   F⁶

E♭: V  I        D:  V⁷  I⁶₄       C:  V²   I⁶

## Exercise C

The nonharmonic tones in this piece are indicated by stars (★). Identify each one by type. **Note:** Some of them may be analyzed in more than one way. Also, it is possible to have a double appoggiatura—two appoggiature on the same beat.

## Chapter Fourteen

# Imitation

Albuquerque, Passamaquoddy, Jacksonville, Albany, Chesapeake Bay. Punxsutawney, Alamagordo, Buffalo, Denver, and Santa Fe. Read these names out loud several times; get the feel of the rhythm of the words. You probably came up with something like the rhythm in Illustration 1.

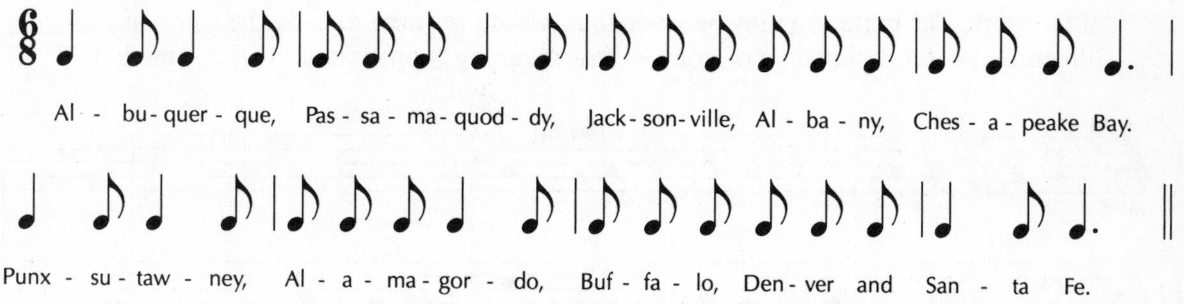

Al - bu - quer - que,   Pas - sa - ma - quod - dy,   Jack - son - ville,   Al - ba - ny,   Ches - a - peake Bay.

Punx - su - taw - ney,   Al - a - ma - gor - do,   Buf - fa - lo,   Den - ver and   San - ta   Fe.

ILLUSTRATION 1

For the next exercise, you'll need at least four people. Read through the above names together until you have the rhythm well established and everyone knows just how it goes. Then read it as a two-part round, two persons per part, as in Illustration 2.

| FIRST READER: | Albuquerque, | Passamaquoddy, | Jacksonville . . . etc. |
| SECOND READER: | (rest) | Albuquerque, | Passamaquoddy . . . etc. |

ILLUSTRATION 2

Once this is done successfully, do the same in four parts with each new part entering a measure after the previous part.

Finally, read the list once more, first in two and then in four parts. Each part should enter a *half* measure after the previous part, as in Illustration 3.

| FIRST READER: | Albuquerque, | Passama—quoddy . . . etc. |
| SECOND READER: | (rest) Albu- | querque, Passama- . . . etc. |

ILLUSTRATION 3

189

When performed in either of these ways, the second, third, and fourth voices are said to be in *imitation* of the first. Composer Ernst Toch wrote a witty example of spoken imitation in his work called "Geographical Fugue." You may want to have a try at creating your own such composition and performing it. You could use automobile names, names of persons, or any other listing of similar items.

## Using Imitation

The principle illustrated above is the simple and familiar technique of musical performance called the *round*. A round, in turn, is a strictly imitative example of a musical form called a *canon*. (**Note:** There is only one *n* in the middle of the word.) A canon is a musical work in which one voice imitates another throughout the duration of the work. The imitation may be *strict*, that is, note for note exactly the same, as in Illustration 4. Or it may be more or less *free*, meaning "approximately the same but

ILLUSTRATION 4

with some amount of variation," as in Illustration 5. Another interesting type of canon

ILLUSTRATION 5

involves imitation at the second (third, fourth, or whatever). In this type of canon every note in the imitating part is a second (third, fourth, or whatever) higher or lower than the corresponding note in the original melody. Illustration 6 is a short canon at the lower second. As we discussed in the last chapter, it is essential in contrapuntal works like these to keep both the vertical harmony and the horizontal melody in mind constantly. Frequently the harmony may dictate the melodic movement.

ILLUSTRATION 6

Before going on with a discussion of imitative forms, it may be well to pause for a moment and discuss the function of imitation in music. Remember that a composer is constantly faced with the problem of getting both unity and variety into a large musical work. One means of achieving this unity is by using the same melodic material in various imitative ways. Variety may also be obtained by using the same material in different ways. Sometimes, as in the canon, the entire piece is organized around imitation of material. Sometimes the imitation is less exact, more fragmented, and other unifying techniques are employed. Whatever the specific piece, though, imitative ideas are common enough to deserve some special attention, and imitative ideas are used to give both unity and variety to a piece of music.

Check your understanding of canons by working Exercise A on Worksheet #15. Have your teacher check your work.

## Renaissance Music

During the historical period known as the High Renaissance (roughly from the time of Columbus until the first English settlements in North America) nearly all European music was based on the principle of imitation. The music of the Roman Catholic Mass, or service of worship, reached its height in the works of two composers, the Spaniard Tomas de la Victoria and the Italian Giovanni da Palestrina. Illustration 7 shows the beginning of the Agnus Dei movement of a Palestrina Mass. Notice how each successive voice repeats, more or less exactly, the voice before it. Notice also that the soprano begins on D, but the alto begins on G with the same melody. Tenor and bass also start on different notes. At any point in the piece after the tenor joins in, you can stop and analyze the harmony in terms of chords, passing tones, anticipations, and so on. This piece is a miracle of imitative writing!

During the Renaissance, instrumental pieces, often called *canzonas* (kan-ZONE-ahs), *ricercars* (RICH-er-kars), or *sonatas* (so-NAH-tahs) were popular. The sonatas and canzonas of Johann Pezel (PET-zel) and Giovanni Gabrieli, published for modern brass ensembles, illustrate these forms well. Imitative sections were usually at the same pitch in canzonas and sonatas, rather than at the dominant, as we saw in the Palestrina vocal example. Frequent changes of meter were typical of the style.

ILLUSTRATION 7

The *madrigal* (MAD-rih-gull) was the favorite secular vocal form, and was often about the sorrows of love. The list of madrigal composers is enormous: Works by William Byrd, Thomas Morley, and Orlando di Lasso are popular with high school madrigal groups. Madrigals are performed by singers, usually in five parts for mixed (male and female) voices. In the Italian madrigal, it was common for the composer to alternate sections in counterpoint with sections in chordal harmony. The excerpt given in Illustration 8 comes from a madrigal by Italian composer Cipriano de Rore, who lived during the early 1500's. This excerpt, which comes from the middle of the piece, has imitative entries on the words, "t'en vai, haime! Sola mi lasci! Adio!" (You are leaving, alas! You leave me alone! Goodbye!). The following words, "che sara qui di me scur'e dolente?" (What will become of me, saddened and sorrowing?) are set basically to a chordal texture. The change of texture from imitation to chordal mode makes a dramatic setting.

ILLUSTRATION 8

# Fugue

Of the musical forms whose basic pattern is imitation, the best-known large form is the fugue (FEW-g). This word comes from the Latin *fuga*, which means "flight." The form began in the 1600's, after the Renaissance, and reached its highest development in the works J. S. Bach in the early 1700's. Reduced to its simplest terms, a fugue consists of alternating the main melody, called the *subject*, with sections that have a different melody, called *episodes*. Illustration 9 shows how a fugue proceeds.

> subject—episode—subject—episode—subject—episode ... subject

ILLUSTRATION 9

A fugue typically begins with the subject, in the soprano, in a section called a *point of imitation*. The term *point* is deceptive since a point of imitation is usually several measures long. The fugue starts with the subject, unaccompanied, in the key of the tonic, as in Illustration 10A. As with rounds, it is easiest to keep track of the action if you think of the fugue as being performed by voices, even though it is usually an instrumental form. This first voice continues with a part that becomes accompaniment when the second voice (alto) enters with the subject. The alto, however, performs the subject in the key of the dominant (as in Illustration 10B) rather than in the tonic. This melody-in-the-dominant-key section is sometimes called the *answer*, as if the first two voices were having a conversation.

These two parts continue with other musical ideas, and soon a third voice (tenor) comes in with the subject, this time in the original key, as in Illustration 10C. Finally, the answer is repeated by the bass in the dominant key, as in Illustration 10D, and the point of imitation is complete.

ILLUSTRATIONS 10A, 10B, 10C, and 10D

During the rest of the fugue, the subject appears in different voices and in different keys. It may appear in just one voice, or in two, three, or more, according to the composer's wishes. The points of imitation may be much shorter and more compact than at the beginning, and all the voices may be in the same key. The composer is free to vary all these things considerably. The last appearance of the subject, however, is always in the tonic key.

The other main element in a fugue is the episode. This is any section in which the subject is not heard. In some fugues, most or all of the episodes have the same melody and constitute a sort of second theme in the composition. This is not usual, however; each episode may have a different melody, or there may be several melodies, some of which are repeated. Illustration 11 shows how an episode may be used contrapuntally with itself.

ILLUSTRATION 11

This, in brief, is a basic description of the fugue. The melodies used here are those of J. S. Bach in his "Little" Fugue in G Minor; listen to this work and try to follow the various parts as described here. Some fugues are more elaborate, having two or more (up to four!) subjects. These are known as double, triple, and quadruple fugues, respectively. All of them follow the general procedures outlined above.

## Other Techniques

Examples of imitation are common in the works of more recent composers. Beethoven, who often took conventional musical ideas to unconventional extremes, exhausted the imitative possibilities in a short four-note motif from his *Symphony No. 5* (quoted in Illustration 12). This dramatic figure provides the whole first theme, plus

ILLUSTRATION 12

other bits and pieces of the symphony. Once more, this demonstrates how imitation and other uses of a strong motif can provide unity in a composition. Illustration 13 is a reduced score of the beginning of the symphony's first movement. Each appearance of the motif is enclosed in arrows.

Later in the symphony, other related ideas pop up. The French horns play a fanfare in the first movement (Illustration 14) that obviously relates to the initial motif.

ILLUSTRATION 13

ILLUSTRATION 14

Still later, in the third movement, the horns blare out another melody (Illustration 15) that keeps the short-short-short-long rhythmic spacing of the famous initial motif. Fragments like this show up in the fourth movement as well.

ILLUSTRATION 15

One fascinating quality of our ability to recognize melodies is that we hear the similarities between melodies with the same rhythmic and tonal patterns even when we turn all the melodic intervals upside down, a process called *inversion*. Illustration 16A is the opening phrase of "The Star Spangled Banner." Illustration 16B is the same melody, with the same rhythm, but with all the intervals of the song inverted. While this inverted version definitely is not the melody played just before kickoff time at a football game, it should be obvious that this version is a variant of that melody, rather than of, say, "God Bless America."

ILLUSTRATIONS 16A and 16B

A melody, then, may be imitated in inversion and still be recognized as the same melody. Johannes Brahms, the nineteenth-century composer whose works were written with such skill and care, often used tricks of inversion. In the third movement of his *Symphony No. 1* he uses a five-measure phrase and its inversion to create the main melody (Illustration 17).

ILLUSTRATION 17

The typical definition of *imitation* suggests that a musical figure is repeated in another voice, starting on the same or different pitch. The unifying character of such imitation is related to the unifying character of a motif used in different ways, as well. Take a piece of music written for band, orchestra, or a choral group which you especially like. Get the condensed score, if possible, and examine it carefully for imitative ideas or "devices." Listen to recordings of those parts to hear, as well as see, how they work out. Then try to use such devices in your own writing. A word of warning: Don't launch into a fugue for your first effort. These are complex works, with their own rules and procedures, and you need some experience with writing music before tackling them. Try something simpler, listen to a performance of your work, and rewrite as you feel is needed. Work to get a piece to sound the way you want it to. That's what writing music is all about.

When you feel you understand the material in this chapter, work Exercise B on Worksheet #15, and have your teacher check the work.

## Exercise A

1. Write a strict canon in $\frac{3}{4}$ meter, not less than four measures long. You may begin the second part on the second or third beat of the first measure, or at the beginning of the second measure.

2. Write a free canon at the interval of a second, third, or fourth. Make it at least four measures long.

## Exercise B

1. The following excerpt is taken from a *ricercar* by Frescobaldi. Using a highlighting pen, mark all imitative sections you find in the work. You may use different color pens for different motifs, if you wish.

2.  Here is a motif whose last note may be any length you choose. Write a sixteen-measure melody using this motif imitatively, both in its original form and in inversion.

## Chapter Fifteen

# Modes, Invented Scales, Parallel Chords, Non-tertian Harmonies

The musical ideas that we have been learning to use—chords, scales, voice leading, functional relationships of chords—are all ideas that were in common use a century ago. These ideas weren't set forth at one time in one place by some god-like super-musician who proclaimed, "Henceforth, music shall abide by *these* rules, forevermore." Instead, they evolved by experiment and improvement over nearly a thousand years of musical practice. What you have been learning is the end product of that millennium of experimentation with musical theory. It has been boiled down and distilled, and the less successful efforts have been omitted. Musical theory can be likened to a giant redwood tree, still drawing on its roots for nourishment, still growing and changing and putting out new branches after a thousand years.

We can carry the tree analogy further. First, the new growth comes out of, and needs the support of, the great trunk that was described in previous pages. No matter how radical a new musical style may sound, its composer must be firmly grounded in the traditions of the music that came before. Second, each new shoot is unique, slightly different from every other on the tree. Some wither and die off, some thrive and become great branches; but each shoot (and each composer) has its own distinctive personality. Third, as with tree shoots, each musical growth is very sensitive to the ecology of its time. Music closely reflects the age and the circumstances in which it is created.

Sometimes new ideas provide the substance of new growth in music; this is true of invented scales and parallel chords. At other times, old ideas are revived or extended in new ways; this is true of modal scales and polytonality. In this chapter, we will examine these and other techniques for expanding your musical vocabulary.

## Modal Scales

In the time of Palestrina, before the present major-minor system of harmony came about, music was based on modes rather than scales. To find out what a mode is, we must look at the white keys of the keyboard. If you play the white keys from C to the next higher C, you think of that as a major scale. The intervals between the notes from C up to C form the pattern we call major. By keeping the intervals constant, we can begin on any key, black or white, and create a major scale. We keep track of the necessary flats or sharps in the key signature. This review is summarized in Illustration 1.

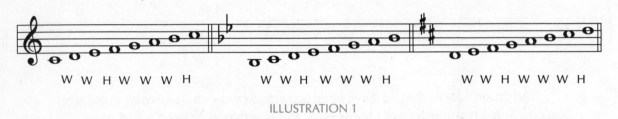

ILLUSTRATION 1

If you play only the white keys from A to the next higher A, you get the intervals of a minor scale. Any scale that has those same intervals is a minor scale, no matter which piano key you begin on. The necessary flats or sharps are recorded at the beginning of the staff, as in Illustration 2.

ILLUSTRATION 2

White key scales beginning on C are major; white key scales beginning on A are minor. But what are the white key scales that begin on one of the other five notes, D, E, F, G, and B? How are these scales different from major and minor? These scales are called *modes*, and they differ in slight but important ways from major and minor scales. In fact, "major scale" and "minor scale" are just different names for two of the modes, although they are harmonized differently from true modal scales.

The C-to-C mode is called the *Ionian* (eye-OWN-ian) mode; it can, of course, be transposed to begin on any pitch, as long as the intervals remain the same. The D-to-D mode is called *Dorian* (DORE-ian). Its intervals resemble the minor scale except for one note: There is a whole step from 5 to 6 and a half step from 6 to 7. This is a small difference, but an important one for writing harmony (Illustration 3).

ILLUSTRATION 3

The E-to-E mode, *Phrygian* (FRIDGE-ian), is another minor-sounding mode, but with a half step between 1 and 2 and another between 5 and 6 (Illustration 4). The

ILLUSTRATION 4

F-to-F mode, *Lydian* (LID-ian), sounds major, but the whole step between 3 and 4 makes an important difference (Illustration 5). The G-to-G mode is called *Mixolydian*

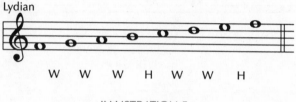

ILLUSTRATION 5

(MIX-oh-LID-ian), and is also a major-sounding mode, but with an interesting minor seventh between the tonic and the leading tone (1 and 7), as seen in Illustration 6.

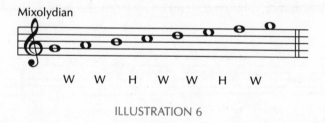

ILLUSTRATION 6

The A-to-A mode, which we usually think of as a minor scale, is the *Aeolian* (ay-OH-lian; "ay" rhymes with "day") mode. Unlike the minor scale, it has only one form, the natural. There are no harmonic or melodic forms, even when harmonizing the scale. Finally, the B-to-B mode, the *Locrian* (LOH-cree-an), sounds minor, but has a diminished fifth between its tonic and dominant. This seldom-used scale appears in Illustration 7.

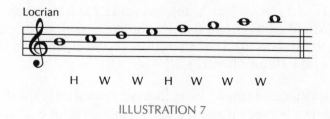

ILLUSTRATION 7

These slight differences in intervallic structure may seem too small to merit discussion. Yet they are quite significant, and their importance is best noted when you consider the chords that result from each mode. We can see this importance if we write the I, IV, and $V^7$ chords in each mode, comparing them to either the major or the minor scale. In Illustration 8, the Dorian scale is compared with the minor scale transposed to begin on D. The three chords appear at the end of each staff. The

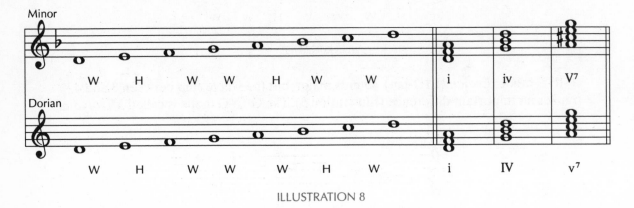

ILLUSTRATION 8

Dorian mode has minor i and $v^7$ chords, but a characteristic major IV; composers often use the progression IV-i to emphasize this quality.

The Phrygian mode is compared with the transposed minor scale in Illustration 9. This mode has a minor i and iv, and a diminished v chord that is difficult to use; because of its dissonance it tends to lead away from the mode. The Lydian mode, with

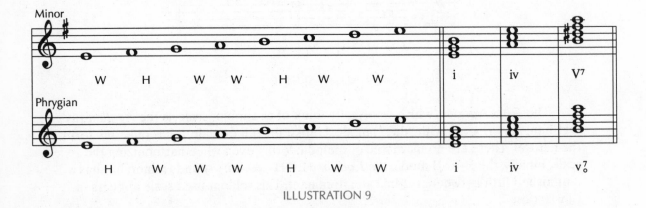

ILLUSTRATION 9

its major sound and its raised fourth step, has major I and V chords. Its iv chord, however, is a diminished triad, and the $V^7$ chord has a major, not a minor, seventh above its root (Illustration 10). The Mixolydian, on the other hand, has major I and IV chords, but a minor v (Illustration 11).

The Aeolian mode, of course, looks like the natural minor scale (Illustration 12). The main difference between it and the minor scale is that the seventh step is never

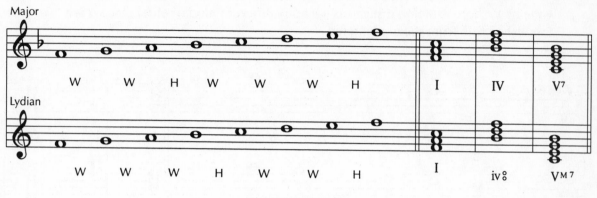

ILLUSTRATION 10

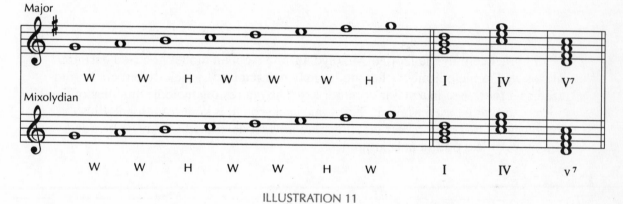

ILLUSTRATION 11

sharped to provide a leading tone; the concept of a leading tone does not fit in modal music. Since its v chord is minor, the progression v-i is seldom used. Instead, a final cadence in Aeolian mode is often VII-i. This whole-step progression is used in several of the minor modes, and, since the Beatles, it has become a fixture in rock music's chord progressions.

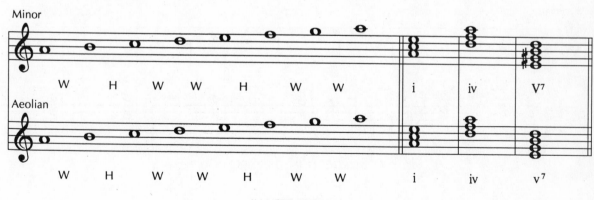

ILLUSTRATION 12

The Locrian mode (Illustration 13) is seldom used; its i is a diminished triad, and while its V chord is major, it suggests a wholly different modal center since it is a diminished fifth from the modal tonic.

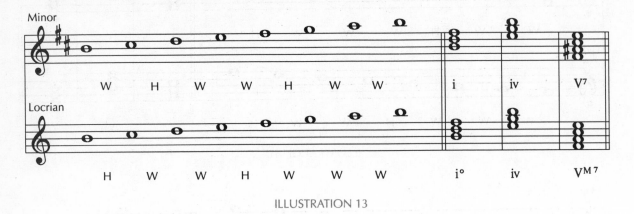

ILLUSTRATION 13

In practice, only the Dorian, Mixolydian, and Aeolian modes are used harmonically as well as melodically. Other modes may be used for the melody, but are harmonized as if they were in a major or minor key. The interesting melodic qualities of the modes can thus be used while the harmonic background is kept traditional. Illustration 14 shows two short pieces that illustrate how modal melodies may be blended with more or less traditional harmonies.

ILLUSTRATIONS 14A and 14B

Hungarian composer Béla Bartók wrote a collection of short pieces for piano, called *Mikrokosmos*, that illustrate many of the things we are discussing in this chapter. Numbers 37 and 55 are in Lydian mode, and number 48 is in Mixolydian. The traditional Irish folk song "Johnny Has Gone for a Soldier" is in Aeolian mode.

The principles of voice leading that apply so strictly in major-minor harmonizations are often altered in modal harmony. Parallel motion of a second or third is often very effective. The principles of chord inversion and of root progressions of a fourth or fifth, however, still apply. Modal harmonizations extend traditional harmony, but do not replace it.

When you have finished this section of the chapter, turn to Worksheet #16 and complete Exercise A. As always, have your teacher check your work when you are done.

## Invented Scales

Of course, one need not stop with novel white key scales. One could invent interesting scales with four, five, six, seven, or more notes per octave that use both black and white keys and that apply harmonies in different ways to the pieces which result. One such "invented" scale (which is actually a common folk music mode in the Middle East) is the "Hungarian minor" scale (which is neither Hungarian nor minor). If based on C, it would have the notes shown in Illustration 15A; its key signature

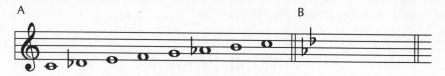

ILLUSTRATIONS 15A and 15B

might be the one shown in 15B. In Bartók's *Mikrokosmos*, number 58 is in the Hungarian minor scale.

One could invent any number of scales to create odd, interesting melodies and harmonies. Illustration 16 shows three possibilities for such scales, and the I, IV, and $V^7$ chords each would produce.

One special type of invented scale was used by Impressionist composers, especially Claude Debussy and Maurice Ravel, around the beginning of the twentieth century. It is called the *whole-tone scale*, and all of its intervals are whole steps (Illustration 17). This scale seems to be in no particular key, and the chords that result are quite different from the usual ones. Used sparingly, this scale can add an exotic touch of color to diatonic music.

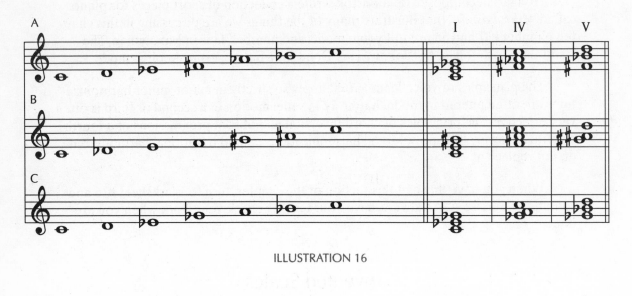

ILLUSTRATION 16

ILLUSTRATION 17

When you have completed this section of the chapter, do Exercise B on Worksheet #16 and have your work checked.

# Parallel Chords

Debussy and Ravel also explored a technique of harmonization called *parallel chords*. One example comes from Debussy's tone poem, "Clouds" (*Nuages*). Illustration 18 is a piano version of one segment of the orchestral score. All the voices move parallel to one another, usually by major seconds or minor thirds. The chords are complex; each is a major chord with a major ninth and minor seventh added. Therefore, they all have the *same degree of dissonance*. This is an important fact, as it allows the chords to flow from one to another without any single chord sounding like a tonic or ending point.

Illustration 19A, also taken from "Clouds," makes use of chords that are not so rigidly parallel, but that all have about the same degree of dissonance. Notice that these seventh chords have the sevenths in the bass and the root in the top voice. At first, they sound like ninth chords, as there is a ninth between the lowest and highest notes. Even triads are used as parallel chords in Debussy's "Clouds" (Illustration 19B).

ILLUSTRATION 18

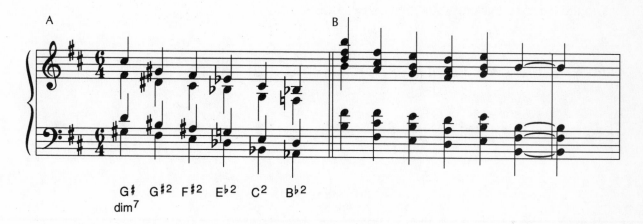

ILLUSTRATIONS 19A and 19B

# Polytonality

A common feature of music since 1900 is the acceptance of greater amounts of dissonance. Some of this dissonance is gained by adding more notes—ninths, elevenths, thirteenths, and so on—to basic triads or seventh chords. In fact, the chord in Illustration 20 can be analyzed in two ways: as a $G^7$ chord with added major ninth, augmented eleventh, and major thirteenth; or as a $G^7$ chord with an A-major chord placed on top of it. In this latter view, we have two keys occurring simultaneously.

If this chord appeared alone in a composition, we would describe it as an extended chord. But if the next several chords were also extended chords in the two keys of G and A, we would think of the chord in Illustration 20 as a *polychord* and say that the music is in two keys at once. Such music is called *polytonal*. A simple example of polytonality would be to write a melody in one key (say, G) and its accompaniment in another key (say, F). The results will sound a bit strange, but not too harsh, except for certain very dissonant intervals where the two keys clash (Illustration 21). The

ILLUSTRATION 20

challenge to the listener is to hear the piece not as a melody with a "wrong" accompaniment, or as an error in transposition, but as an expansion of the abilities of the mind and ear to follow musical action on two tracks at once.

ILLUSTRATION 21

French composer Darius Milhaud (dar-YOU mee-YOH) sometimes used polytonality in his music. In a piece for piano he called "Copacabana," he wrote the melody part in the key of B major, but the harmony in G major. The result is an intriguing, spicy *samba* with a very modern sound. In Illustration 22A, the samba is written all in the key of G; pretty, but not very memorable. In Illustration 22B is the same samba as Milhaud wrote it. The effect of polytonality is unforgettable.

Sometimes two keys are mingled in one series of *superchords* so that the chords are not obviously polytonal, but they remain quite dissonant. In Illustration 23A, the left hand plays an $F^7$ chord while the right plays a D-flat chord. If one intermixes the notes as in Illustration 23B, the result is a very dense and dissonant chord of uncertain key. A series of such superchords would be very dissonant, but the polytonal nature of the chords would not be apparent.

## Non-tertian Chords

Conventional harmonizations are based on chords made of thirds, or *tertian chords*. In the twentieth century, composers have experimented with chords based on intervals other than the third. We have already seen a beginning step in this direction

ILLUSTRATIONS 22A and 22B

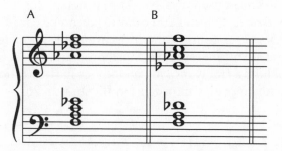

ILLUSTRATIONS 23A and 23B

through the use of ninths, elevenths, and thirteenths, as in Illustration 24A. If you move all the notes above F in this chord down an octave, the result is a very dense chord made up entirely of seconds, as in Illustration 24B. Such a chord is called a *tone cluster*. Tone clusters usually have three or more notes, but not necessarily seven. Not all the seconds in tone clusters need be adjacent; you can have spaces of a third, fourth, or some other interval between groups of seconds, as in Illustration 24C. In Bartók's *Mikrokosmos*, number 63 is harmonized entirely in seconds.

If seconds may be used instead of thirds, then why not fourths or fifths? Sixths, of course, are simply inverted thirds and therefore sound tertian. But if we can use seconds, fourths, and fifths, how about sevenths? Obviously, such harmonies are entirely possible and do result in some startling effects. Composers use harmony in fourths ("quartal" harmony) or fifths ("quintal" harmony). Aaron Copland's well-known *Fanfare for the Common Man* is based on quartal harmonies. There are many other examples, as well.

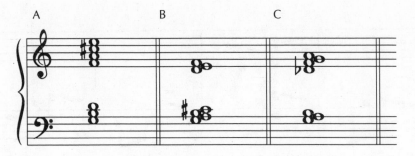

ILLUSTRATIONS 24A, 24B, and 24C

Béla Bartók, in the second movement of his *Concerto for Orchestra*, sums up these experiments in a tongue-in-cheek display of writing skill. The movement consists mainly of a series of duets for various instruments. First come two bassoons, harmonized in sixths. Next, two oboes play a new melody harmonized in thirds. These are followed by two clarinets in sevenths, two flutes in fifths, and two trumpets in seconds. After a middle section, the same series of duets is then repeated with some elaboration. Listen to this witty and charming piece, following the score if possible.

Of course, non-triadic harmonization is not restricted to duets. American composer William Schuman used massive tone clusters in his work for band entitled *George Washington Bridge*. Quartal and quintal harmonies are fairly common in the twentieth century, too. Often fourths and fifths are used simply to create new background sounds rather than generate new chord progressions from them. These chords may be sustained behind a freely moving melody, as in Illustration 25. They may also be used as rhythmically repeated chords, as in Illustration 26.

ILLUSTRATION 25

Much more can be said about the techniques described in this chapter, and many more techniques are used in twentieth-century music. However, it is the purpose of this text to introduce you to traditional harmony, and to get you started in the fascinating and rewarding practice of writing your own original music and hearing it played. Once you have mastered this much, you will be ready to go on to further study of composition and arranging at a more advanced level.

ILLUSTRATION 26

When you feel ready, do Exercise C on Worksheet #16, and have your teacher check your work.

## Exercise A

1. On the lines below these four versions of the song "Yankee Doodle," identify the modes used.

2. Harmonize the following sections of modal melodies, using one chord at each asterisk (*).

A

B

## Exercise B

Here is the melody to "America." Write it three times: first, using the "Hungarian minor" scale; second, using the whole tone scale; and third, using a scale of your own invention (NOT a mode). Play the results over and evaluate them; ask yourself how you could use these versions in a composition.

### Exercise C

1. Here is the melody to the Welsh song "The Ash Grove," with indicated chords. On the bass staff, create an accompanying part in another key.

2. The excerpt below is from the folk song "Bound for the Promised Land." Make a vocal arrangement of it (SAB or SATB) using quartal or quintal harmonies. You need not create a chord for each melody note, and you may invert your chords. You may wish to do this assignment on separate manuscript paper and to have a group sing your arrangement.

## Chapter Sixteen

# Analyzing Musical Scores

You are now at a point in your study of musical theory where you can, with a little help, become your own teacher. You know how the basic language of music works. You have the tools to study how composers use that language and to learn how to use it yourself in a creative way, either by arranging music or by writing your own. Your next step is to begin looking at written music—thousands of examples of it—and taking it apart to see what makes it tick. From such study and analysis, you can learn how Chopin's music is different from Beethoven's, or how Stephen Sondheim's is different from Peter Townshend's.

In this chapter, we will discuss some methods that will help you make sense of someone else's music. It is not necessary for you to follow these steps in the order indicated; find your own style of studying composers' scores. It is probably best, however, for you to begin as suggested here: by listening, closely and several times, to the music you want to analyze.

## Importance of Listening

The written score is, after all, only a means of showing a performer how to re-create a musical composition. While it has all the details on the page, there is a danger that, by studying the score alone, you will become so involved with the trees that you will miss the forest. Your ears can provide you with the best assessment, not only of the qualities of a work, but of what the overall plan of the work is like.

It will be most helpful if you can listen with the written score in front of you. You may wish to photocopy your "study score," so that you can write on it without marking up the original. Later on, you may wish to actually copy the original over by hand, noting how the composer achieved the effects he or she did. Listen to the work several times, each time with certain points in mind; make notes on the score about what you noticed during each listening. Begin by getting an overall sense of the piece. What is the key? Does it change, and if it does, for how long? What are the main melodic ideas (label them A, B, etc.) that appear in the piece? Is the mood consistent, or does it change as the piece progresses? Is the overall work in a simple form—AB, ABA, AABA—or some other form?

Next, listen for harmonic change. How long does one basic chord seem to last before a change occurs? Do the chord changes take place in a rhythmic pattern, for example, every measure, twice a measure, or some other scheme? If a melody recurs, is the harmony basically the same, or are there fundamental differences? Don't try to analyze too deeply yet; you are still seeking an overview of the piece as a whole.

Now listen again for devices we have discussed in this text. Are there sections of imitation in the piece? Sequences? Does the harmony sound like parallel chords or special scales or modes? Is the chordal texture thick, or do most of the chords seem to be triads?

If you have done the above, you probably have several of the melodies in mind firmly enough to hum along when the piece is played. You are now ready to move on to the next phase of score analysis.

## Reducing to Basics

With your listening notes written on the score, you're now ready to examine the notation in more detail. For some pieces it may be useful to begin with a harmonic analysis; for others, you may wish to start by looking for devices that will clarify what happens in the harmony. Either approach can be useful; for now, let's assume that you are beginning with harmonic analysis.

Musical scores can be confusing; there are so many notes, so much going on at once, that it is hard to make sense of the music. If you block out basic harmonic motion by listening, however, the task becomes much simpler. Many of the notes probably have to do with keeping a rhythmic pulse going through the piece. In Illustration 1A, for instance, which is the first eight measures of the "Notre Dame Victory March," the melody moves in slow notes, mostly whole and half notes, while the accompaniment moves in short, choppy rhythms to propel the piece forward. In Illustration 1B, the rhythm parts are reduced to block chords that account for the actual harmonic motion of the piece. Study these two scores carefully to see how they match and where they differ.

The higher notes on the treble staff of Illustration 1A are the melody part; the lower notes are a countermelody, such as might be found in a baritone part. The bass staff contains a rhythmic harmony part. The harmonic reduction in Illustration 1B shows the basic chords and their Roman numerals below the melody notes. The countermelody in measure 4 begins on a chord tone (C) and connects, by passing tones, to a chord tone in measure 5 (E). There is no need to analyze the D and D-sharp as a major ninth and an augmented ninth, respectively, although such an analysis wouldn't be wrong. Notice that the countermelody's motion in measure 4 occurs while the melody has a whole note, thereby adding rhythmic interest to an otherwise static point

ILLUSTRATION 1A

in the song. In measure 8 the bass also has a nonharmonic tone, the G, which is simply a passing tone between two chord tones.

ILLUSTRATION 1B

Some of the numbered chords in Illustration 1B do not exactly accord with the letter-named chords; the V in measure 2, for instance, and the F dim in measure 7. The point to be considered here is that the overall effect of these chords is indicated by the Roman numeral. In measure 2, it is not important that the V is an augmented chord; similarly, in measure 7, the whole measure is harmonized by a I chord, even if at one moment the chord is diminished. Block out harmonizations in broad terms like this; you can later decide if it is appropriate to fill in the details.

## Special Devices and Effects

Once the harmonic structure of a piece is sketched out, you should go through the piece looking for some of the special qualities we have discussed in this book. One special device that should be easily observed is *imitation*. If a work has substantial imitative sections in it, you have a clue as to the nature of the whole work. Perhaps it is a fugue, or perhaps it is a work from before 1750. If so, you may also be on the alert for examples of *augmentation* or *diminution*, two techniques that were common in music of that period. You may also look for examples of *inversion* in such pieces.

At a glance, it is obvious that Illustration 2, an excerpt from Bach's "Contra-punktus VII" (from *The Art of the Fugue*), is imitative in texture.. In measure 1 the

ILLUSTRATION 2

basic melody appears in the tenor; in measure 2, the same melody, inverted and augmented, is in the soprano. In measure 3, the soprano's part is imitated by the alto in diminution. Beginning in measure 5, the inverted tenor melody appears in double augmentation in the bass. Surely, this is a musical tour de force.

How different is the texture of Illustration 3! Here we have a portion of a popular song from many years ago. The dense, lush *extended chords* create a special mood utterly unlike Bach's piece. Notice how the thick-textured chords still keep a strong functional relationship to one another; we can easily assign chord numbers here.

ILLUSTRATION 3

Another device that can usually be seen at a glance is the *sequence*. Illustration 4 is taken from the first movement of Mozart's *Symphony No. 40*. Mozart uses the sequence section to move from one key to another; it is easy to spot the repetition of the melodic idea as it moves downward over several measures.

In the last chapter, we discussed the use of *parallel harmony*, a technique particularly common in Impressionist music. Once more, it is easy to pick out the section where all the voices move in the same direction at the same time. Often, as in Illustration 5, a number of accidentals are involved in parallel harmonizations.

If you feel you understand the material covered so far in this chapter, work the problems in section A of Worksheet #17, and have your teacher check the results.

ILLUSTRATION 4

ILLUSTRATION 5

# Significance of Accidentals

Parallel harmony is one possible source of accidentals in a composition; wherever accidentals show up, you know that the basic key is being modified in some way, often for a sustained period of time. If the accidentals appear in only one or two chords, you may suspect that the composer has used a secondary dominant, a Neapolitan or augmented sixth chord, or perhaps a diminished seventh for color effects or to make a brief modulation. If the accidentals occur over a lengthy span of measures, this suggests that a new key has been established for a time, or perhaps that there is a chromatic passage in the music.

If there are only a few accidentals, begin your analysis by looking at the notes that are modified. If the same pitch is raised frequently in the piece, you may suspect that it is in *minor mode.* In Illustration 6, the C is consistently sharped; the last chord is a d-minor chord, and C-sharp is the leading tone of d minor.

When analyzing chords with accidentals, it is often useful to begin by looking at the chord(s) after the one with the accidental, to see how they relate to the altered chord. If one pitch is altered several times, but not throughout the work, you may

ILLUSTRATION 6

have a *temporary modulation*. Illustration 7 is taken from a Bach chorale, with the harmonization simplified for clarity. On the last beat of the first measure a pivot chord changes the key from A to E. On the third beat of the third measure, another pivot chord returns the key to the original A.

ILLUSTRATION 7

When accidentals appear on various pitches in a chord progression, check to see if they result from a string of *secondary dominants*. Part of an old popular song, "Harrigan," is quoted in Illustration 8. Notice that the accidentals that appear here are secondary dominants. They are not modulating chords because the changes of key last for only one chord, and the series of chords returns to the original key at the end.

ILLUSTRATION 8

Sometimes you will find a single chord with accidentals; it may or may not be a pivot chord, again depending on what follows the altered chord. If the following chords are within the original key, the modified chord could be a Neapolitan sixth or one of the augmented sixth chords. In Illustration 9, a Neapolitan sixth chord gives extra flavor to an otherwise quite commonplace progression at the end of the second movement of Vivaldi's *Concerto Grosso in D minor*, Op. 3, No. 11.

ILLUSTRATION 9

Accidentals may also result from *changes of mode* (major to minor, or vice versa), which may in turn be used as modulating chords. Jazz musicians enjoy the challenge of improvising on the song called "Laura" because of the complex key changes in a short space of time. Many of these result from modal changes in the melody (Illustration 10).

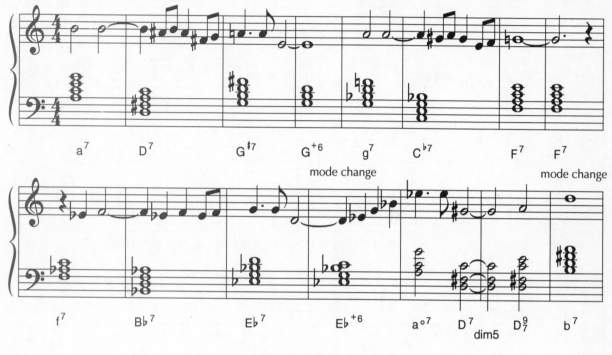

ILLUSTRATION 10

Of course, accidentals will occur when a *diminished seventh chord* is used. Study the example in Illustration 11, which is taken from the last movement of Haydn's String Quartet Op. 76, No. 3. The diminished seventh chords appear in the fourth and sixth measures of this segment. Notice, also, that this excerpt ends with a long pedal point in the cello part—still another device for which you can look during a score analysis. Pedal points are particularly revealing since they usually end in a structurally important cadence in the piece.

Finally, you must never lose sight of the fact that music is *sounds*, not theoretical abstractions. Illustration 12 is taken from the beginning of Chopin's Prélude No. 4. The second measure begins with what might be a $V^7$ chord with a nonharmonic suspended E, and in mid-measure changes to what *sounds like* a $V^7$ chord. Chopin lets us know, however, that this is not his intended chord, for he uses an E-flat rather than a D-sharp. Why isn't this a dominant chord? Because it doesn't resolve in a conventional way. Instead, Chopin is exploring the possibilities in gradual chromatic alterations of chords, one voice at a time. The result is a marvelously expressive work that defies conventional analysis.

After reviewing the material pertaining to accidentals, do Exercise B on Worksheet #17. See if you can identify the techniques used in this excerpt from a musical score. As always, have your teacher check your work.

ILLUSTRATION 11

ILLUSTRATION 12

## Exercise A

The following score is taken from the first movement of Haydn's String Quartet in C Major, Op. 76, No. 3. Write chord numbers beneath all the chords. Also, point out any special compositional techniques, discussed in this book, that you find here.

## Exercise B

The following excerpt is taken from Schumann's "Papillons" (Butterflies). Write the chord numbers beneath the chords, and look for any other compositional techniques used in the piece. One hint: There is a brief pedal point in the bass somewhere in this piece.

# Appendix A:
# Arranging for Vocal Groups

Music is a performer's art. It does not exist on the printed page. Music is in the air because an artful musician sings or plays it according to a composer's written instructions. Although a painter or sculptor can stand back and admire his or her product, the composer with a completed score must find a performer or group to make the music a reality.

The composer who has access to professional performers has considerable freedom as to what to write; he or she can try complex or difficult things and expect that the group will make the written music sound as good as possible, however clumsily written. Amateur groups may not be so skilled, though. The composer or arranger must take special pains to write music that will sound good even when performed by less skillful groups.

The human voice normally takes over twenty years to mature; this fact imposes certain limits on the range and difficulty of music written for high school groups, whose voices are still forming. Composers of high school vocal music should write parts within a practical range—one that most singers can achieve confidently without creating undue strain on the voice. Estimates of high school students' ranges vary; those given in Illustration 1 are fairly conservative. The arranger may exceed them for a few notes of brief duration, especially if he or she knows the capabilities of individual singers.

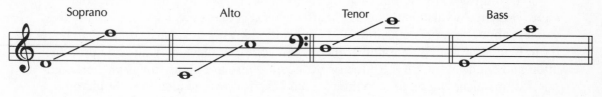

ILLUSTRATION 1

Even within these ranges, the parts will sound best if the top and bottom pitches are used sparingly. **Special Note**: Arranging for junior high or young high school students presents special problems. (See page 240.)

Certain intervals should probably be avoided for high school students. Singers have long called the augmented fourth/diminished fifth twins the "Devil in music" because they are difficult to perform accurately and in tune. Test this on yourself. Play F on the piano and sing it. Now try to sing B natural above or below the F, without sounding the note beforehand. Check your accuracy by playing the B while singing it. Now go the other way: start with the B, and try to sing the F. These intervals are even more difficult to sing accurately when other voices have different notes at the same time. Avoid having your compositional masterpiece destroyed by tenors who must grope for the right pitch, with varying success. Stay away from augmented fourths and diminished fifths in any one part.

Other intervals are also difficult to hear in advance. Major sevenths (C up to B, for example) and intervals greater than an octave are apt to produce faulty intonation. All augmented intervals (seconds, thirds, fifths, and so on) may better be written enharmonically, even though the spelling may not be correct for the chord used. In Illustration 2, the tenor part illustrates how an awkward part can be rewritten to improve its singability.

ILLUSTRATION 2

The acid test for vocal music is, of course, how easily it can be sung. Ideally, each part should be reasonably logical and melodic. It is good practice for you to try to sing through every part you write and make necessary changes to improve the smoothness or logical flow of each line. Remember that bass parts customarily jump around by intervals of a fourth or larger, but other parts are much less active in intervals. This "sing-through" approach applies equally well to instrumental music, though the problem isn't as critical with instruments as it is for vocal music.

Vocal music contains one major element that instrumental music does not, namely, a text. Any listener who has heard a choral concert given by a group that was careless about both pronunciation and enunciation knows how frustrating it can be to try to figure out what an unfamiliar piece is all about. While achieving good pronunciation and enunciation are the director's concern, there are many things an alert composer or arranger can do to help things along. The following guidelines should be observed.

1. In general, *singers sing vowels, not consonants.* A, E, I, O, U, and their combinations (called *diphthongs;* the vowels in "toil") and various pronunciations (far, cat, may) are the basic tone colors of vocal music. Vowels are supplemented and separated (or articulated) by various consonantal sounds: hisses ("s" and "z," mostly); pops ("p," "t," "b," "d"); glottals ("k," "g," "q"); nasal bagpipe sounds ("m," "n"); softer airy sounds made by lips and teeth ("f," "v"), or in the throat ("h"); as well as less definable sounds such as "j," "l," "r," "w," "x," "y," and the "ch" sound as in the German word *ach.*

In most cases, the meaning of the words is more important than the musical setting. The composer wants the words to be heard and clearly understood. Unfortunately, English is not always an easy language to enunciate clearly, partly because the singer sometimes runs into awkward clumps of consonants that challenge the tongue's athletic skills. Thomas Jefferson displayed a musician's feeling for singable prose (he was himself a competent musician): "We hold these truths to be self-evident, that all men are created equal, that they are endowed by their Creator with certain unalienable Rights, that among these are Life, Liberty, and the pursuit of Happiness." Compare such a liquid sentence with the following translation from Thomas Aquinas: "Mathematical species can be abstracted intellectually not only from individual sensible matter but also from the common matter—not from common intelligible matter but only from the individual." Not merely the meaning of this sentence, but each and every syllable, tumbles clumsily behind one's teeth.

Compare these sentences to discover why one would be more singable than the other. Remember that one *sings* vowels and *articulates* consonants. If we transcribe Jefferson's text as it would be sung, it would look something like this: "Wee ho-old-thee-ztroo-thzto bee sel-fe-vi-dent," and so on. The consonants are crowded up against each other, the vowels prolonged. Omit all the consonants and consider just the vowels of the first seven words for a moment. The following is the result: "ee-o, ee-oo, ee-eh." These sounds form a pattern and a progression. They immediately suggest a musical setting.

Now look at the clusters of consonants. The first group, "-ldth-," (in "hold these") is a bit of a challenge, but the tongue stays at the front of the mouth. It can roll fairly smoothly through the group without tying in knots. In the rest of the sentence, all the other consonant clusters flow quite smoothly. Try them out, one by one, saying them slowly to discover how smoothly they run together.

Now turn to the sentence from Aquinas. Considering vowels alone, there is much greater variety, more choppiness, no pattern of progression: "(M)a(th)eh(m)a(t)ih-(c)a(l) (sp)ee(c)ee(z) (c)a(n) (b)ee a(bstr)a(ct)eh(d)," etc. The consonant clusters are formidable: "lsp" (from "-ical spec-") rolls from the palate out to the lips; "nb" (from "can be") is always clumsy; and "bstr" (from "abstracted) is nearly unsingable.

Selection of text, therefore, is quite important. Given a good, singable text that does not pose too many problems of articulation for the singers, you can go on to create an effective setting.

2. *The music must not obscure the words.* Block chord settings, such as hymns or some folk songs, are effective because everybody sings the same word at the same time. The safest course is seldom the most interesting, however. Too much block chord music, as in Illustration 3, guarantees a sleeping audience. The trick, then, is to be clear and yet interesting at the same time. One way to add clarity and interest to basically chordal harmonizations is to write slightly different rhythmic parts for the accompanying voices so that the words don't coincide precisely in all parts, as in Illustration 4. Sometimes you can use a point of imitation or canonic effect in one verse of a song, as in Illustration 5.

Another effective technique is to score rapid notes in unison or octaves and longer notes as chords, as in Illustration 6. In each of these cases, the arrangement is

ILLUSTRATION 3

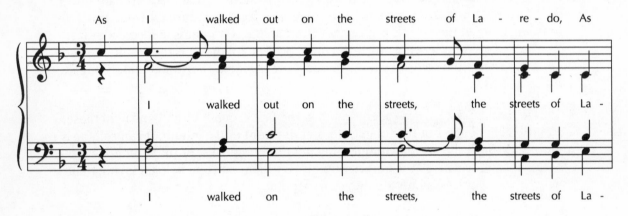

ILLUSTRATION 4

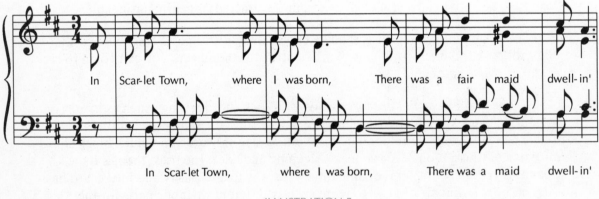

ILLUSTRATION 5

given some interest, while the words are not obscured by having too many things going on at once.

ILLUSTRATION 6

3. *Keep all parts relatively simple.* Try to approximate the patterns of speech in each musical phrase. Avoid complicated rhythm patterns and long series of rapid notes. Even when many rapid notes are sung on only one syllable, as in Illustration 7, the result is apt to sound either like a long, uncontrolled wail or like a nervous stammer: "hohohohohohohohold." Neither effect improves the clarity of the text.

ILLUSTRATION 7

Vocal groups are of three types: all male, all female, and mixed voices. All-male and all-female groups usually have two (SA, TB), three (SSA, TTB, or TBarB), or four (SSAA, TTBB) parts to their music. If you consult the vocal ranges given earlier in Illustration 1, you can easily see that writing four parts for all-male or all-female groups calls for some squeezing together of parts within a narrow range, or a great deal of doubling parts on certain notes. Generally, it is easier to write just two or three parts for like voices. For SATB writing, four parts work out well, if the performers have the needed skill and balance of parts. Grouping all the boys together on one lower part (SAB) is an alternative if the number of females greatly exceeds the number of males in the group.

Choirs sometimes specialize in one particular style of music. The madrigal group, for example, performs mainly the music of sixteenth- and seventeenth-century composers. More recently, swing choirs and barbershop quartets have extended the repertoire in new directions, performing specialized types of popular music. Writing for a swing choir requires the use of some special harmonic techniques, some of which are described in Appendix C.

Since you will be writing your own ideas in the future, it's difficult to suggest how to arrange your parts. The best way to learn is to listen to and study the scores of many pieces by published composers and arrangers. Some will be good, some not so good; you can learn from both. You should analyze pieces to discover what you personally like or dislike. Don't hesitate to imitate an arranger whose work you like; such imitation will help you mold your own style.

Here are some general comments about writing for vocal groups. The simplest scoring, obviously, is unison or octave writing. The effect is dramatic, and the text is clearly heard. When mixed voices are scored in multiple octaves, as in Illustration 8, the effect may be either comical or, if done slowly and softly, strange and eerie. As a momentary effect, such scoring can be dramatic, but it lacks color and interest if prolonged.

ILLUSTRATION 8

Two-part harmonizing in thirds, sixths, or tenths is light and "folky" in sound. Spanish or Italian songs are often done in this fashion, as in Illustration 9. Scoring in parallel fourths or fifths gives a hollow, medieval quality to the music. Our culture has a hard time listening to (or singing!) music written in parallel sevenths or seconds.

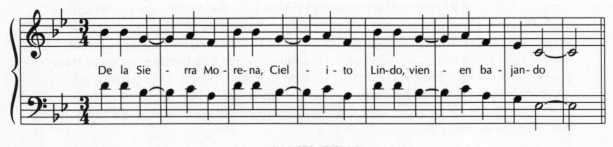

ILLUSTRATION 9

When reducing four-part writing to three parts, the voice usually omitted is the wide-ranging bass part, even if the arranger is scoring for TBarB. These arrangements are written (transposed to the proper register, of course) as if they were the top three parts (SAT) of a traditional four-part selection, as in Illustration 10. However, you need to be sure that you have all the necessary notes and decent voice leading. Notice that the tenor in this illustration is written in treble clef. Tenor parts are often written

ILLUSTRATION 10

an octave higher than they will actually sound. This is to save the copyist from writing ledger lines for nearly every note, making the part hard to read. The numeral 8 below the treble clef indicates that all the pitches will be an octave below the written notes.

Four-part music is usually scored in one of two ways: in "close position" (that is, with all adjacent notes near one another, as in Illustration 11A), or in "open position" (that is, with wider distances between adjacent notes, as in Illustration 11B). Close scoring gives a feeling of tight togetherness and density when well performed. Close scoring is easier to sing in tune and is effective at all volume levels; swing choir arrangements are typically scored in close position. Open scoring can sound more grandiose, majestic, and sometimes pompous, but there are apt to be intonation problems and one part is usually singing near the extreme of the range. In many styles of music, the texture alternates between close and open position.

ILLUSTRATIONS 11A and 11B

Contrapuntal writing, in which each voice has its own melodic part, as in a fugue, gives a marvelous feeling of motion and "busyness," but makes the text harder for the audience to follow. Counterpoint also takes more skill to write well than melody-plus-chord arrangements.

Writing solo parts is a tricky business because you must arrange for the solo voice to project over the mass of the chorus. Often the chorus part will be hummed or sung on a neutral syllable like "oo," which will allow a strong solo voice to predominate. Good strong solo voices are not that common in high school choirs, so you should know the capabilities of the singers for whom you are writing.

Finally, musical settings should always support the sense of the words. If the text is a lament, for example, you will want to consider a minor mode setting because, in our culture, minor keys are associated with sadness. You may decide to not use minor for your own reasons; the contrast between sorrowful text and major sonority can be a very effective device. However, you should probably begin by thinking through the possibilities offered by a minor modality.

Composers often use what is called text painting where appropriate. In text painting, the musical line illustrates the sense of the words. For instance, if the text mentions "high" or "sky" or "rising," the musical setting will use a high note or an ascending scale for these words. Similarly, "low," "deep," or "down" might be set by appropriately low notes. These simple and naive examples by no means exhaust the possibilities of text painting. George Frideric Handel's ever-popular oratorio *Messiah* is full of such musical puns. To give but one example, Handel sets part of the following text as shown in Illustration 12: "Thus saith the Lord of Hosts: Yet once a little while and I will shake the heavens and the earth, the sea and the dry land, and I will shake all nations." The word *shake* is repeated several times, and each time it is set to a teeth-rattling string of sixteenth notes. By the way, notice that the note for the word *earth* is lower than that for *heavens*—of course!

ILLUSTRATION 12

Arranging for junior high school vocal groups presents a number of special problems. First, the ranges of the voices are somewhat narrower than for high school students. Most such groups lack true altos and basses, and the tenors are apt to be thin in quality and rather uncertain of upper and lower notes. The male voice does not settle firmly into its adult range until high school or beyond, in most cases. Furthermore, both boys and girls undergo a voice change during which their voices deepen and darken in quality, but the change is much more evident and nerve-wracking for boys. Some arrangers write special parts for boys undergoing this transformation, usually called alto-tenor or *cambiata* parts. Such parts should be kept to the narrow range of notes shown in Illustration 13; notes above and below this range will probably be quite insecure. As it may take months for boys to pass through the voice change, which may occur at any age from twelve to sixteen, learning to write cambiata parts may be quite useful to anyone writing for these groups. For guidance, discuss any works you may wish to do with the group's director.

JUNIOR HIGH SCHOOL RANGES

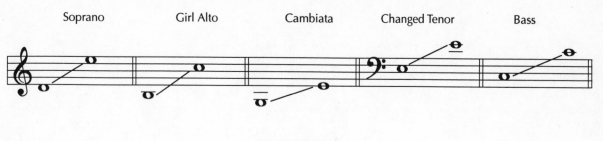

ILLUSTRATION 13

These few comments about writing music for voices are, certainly, only a bare introduction. You will learn much more from examining well-written choral music, from singing it through part by part, from performing in choral ensembles, and—not least!—from writing and then hearing your own material. However, if you keep within the practical ranges of your singers, stress clarity of text, and look for opportunities to use fresh ideas in your writing, you should be able to do quite successful arrangements or compositions for high school vocal groups. Write music you can get excited about; it's the only kind that's worth performing!

For further instruction in scoring music for vocal ensembles, you may wish to study the following book: *Choral Arranging*, by Hawley Ades, Delaware Water Gap, PA: Shawnee Press, 1966. You may also want to consult the chapter on scoring for vocal groups with instrumental backgrounds in this book: *Music Arranging and Orchestration*, by John Cacavas, Melville, NY: Belwin-Mills Publishing Corp., 1975.

# Appendix B:
## Arranging for Instrumental Groups

Arranging or writing for instrumental groups offers the composer a smorgasbord of tasty sounds to sample. In addition to the grandiose sonorities of band and orchestra, you may choose from a wide variety of smaller groups for which to write: brass, woodwind, or string choirs; brass, flute, clarinet, or saxophone trios, quartets, or quintets; clarinet choirs; string quartets; woodwind quintets; percussion ensembles, to name but a few. You could also write for less standard groupings such as flute, oboe, and bassoon; or clarinet, cello, and piano. The possibilities are limited only by the writer's imagination.

In smaller groups, each instrument usually plays a melodic part; even such unusual instruments as snare drums may have a featured role to play. In larger groups, however, instruments usually play one of several roles—melody, countermelody, harmony, rhythm, or "special effects." These roles are not mutually exclusive; a harmony instrument in one measure may become a melody instrument a few measures later. Nevertheless, these various functions are usually heard in any piece, and certain instruments tend to end up in one of these roles. Let's examine the roles one by one, and see how various instruments fit into them.

*Melody parts* most commonly appear in the treble register, less frequently in the upper bass register. *Countermelodies* are usually found in the low treble or high bass registers and less often in the high treble. *Harmony* and *rhythmic parts* also tend to fall in the low treble/high bass registers, though exceptions to this may be quite dramatic in effect. Rhythmic parts are often divided between tubas (low bass) and French horns, saxophones, or trombones (low treble). Special effects instruments include tamtam, castanets, guiro, maracas, and others whose purpose is to add special colors to the sound rather than to serve one of the basic functions.

Certain instruments play mainly in the extreme registers above the treble staff or below the bass staff. The main function of such instruments is coloristic. The instruments playing above the treble staff usually duplicate the melody within the staff, giving it added brilliance. Instruments that play below the bass staff give an organlike power and majesty to the regular bass part. Few instruments play in these registers with any regularity, though some, like the piccolo or the contrabass clarinet, are most effective in these extreme registers.

Most percussion instruments are unpitched and fit into no specific register. Their sounds, however, generally fall into either the bass or the treble range. Snare and bass drums, for example, tune to bass-register pitches, whereas instruments such as the triangle and tambourine fall into the treble register. Pitched percussion instruments, of course, play specific notes in the bass or treble staff.

At the end of this appendix, common band and orchestra instruments are listed, together with their practical ranges, transpositions, and comments about their use. The instruments are arranged in *score order*, the way they are customarily written in a full score. Score order is by family, with each family arranged from highest to lowest: first the woodwinds, then the brass, then percussion, and finally the strings. All your arranging for large instrumental groups should be done in score order. For smaller groups, arrange the score in SATB order, regardless of instrument or family. Remember that if you are writing a piece for band, you will have no string parts, whereas if you are writing for orchestra, there will be neither saxophones nor baritones.

By custom, certain types of instruments are given several parts within the type. Clarinets and cornets, for example, are often written in two or three different parts (first, second, and perhaps third clarinet or cornet) in band scoring. When arranging for clarinet quartet (three sopranos and bass), the first plays the soprano part, the second the alto, and the third the tenor, with the bass clarinet rounding out the ensemble. A brass quartet of three cornets and a baritone would be scored in a similar manner, as would three trombones and a tuba. A saxophone quartet (two altos, tenor, and baritone) would divide the two altos between soprano and alto parts. In a string quartet, violins are divided into 1sts and 2nds playing soprano and alto parts, with the viola playing the tenor and the cello the bass.

When writing for larger groups, bands or orchestras, there are a number of conventions about instrument parts. In smaller groups, flutes, oboes, and bassoons have one part each, but in larger groups there may be two parts for each instrument. When writing for orchestra, trumpets, clarinets, and trombones are customarily given either two or three parts each. French horns are often scored for band or orchestra in four parts (SATB) with one major difference. Historically, French horn parts are distributed with first horn playing soprano, second playing tenor, third part alto, and the fourth the bass; if there are fewer than four parts, the bass is the first part to be left out. As in the string quartet, violins are divided between 1sts and 2nds, while other strings have one part each. All other instruments (alto and bass clarinets, baritones, tubas, etc.) have one written part each.

Simple, hymn-like SATB scoring is one of several standard types of arranging for instruments; it is often referred to as *block scoring*. Chorales and patriotic songs are often arranged in block scoring. Instruments are assigned to the various voice parts which are then written out in the transposed key. Illustration 1A shows an SATB, or

ILLUSTRATION 1A

block-scored, arrangement of the beginning of "America, the Beautiful"; Illustration 1B shows the same SATB arrangement as it might be scored for band. Notice that the

ILLUSTRATION 1B

melody is written in two octaves for baritone, oboe, flute, 1st clarinet, 1st cornet, and 1st alto saxophone; the harmonization also occurs in at least two octaves. The fourth French horn part would double the third where there are only three pitches in the score. All the lowest instruments—bass clarinet, baritone sax, bassoon, tuba—reinforce the bass part.

A second type of arranging is called *march style* because it follows the usual pattern used for military march music. In march style, the instruments are usually assigned parts according to the various functions mentioned earlier: melody, countermelody, harmony, rhythm, and special effects. There may also be a special type of countermelody called an *obbligato* melody. Let's look briefly at a few bars from John Philip Sousa's immortal march "The Stars and Stripes Forever" to see these various parts in action.

Rare is the American who does not recognize this famous melody, played first by the baritone and in later repetitions by the cornets as well (Illustration 2). Meanwhile,

ILLUSTRATION 2

what is the *rest* of the band doing? Sousa gave the piccolo players one of the most celebrated solos in the repertoire. The jaunty tune in Illustration 3 is called the obbligato part. This isn't the main melody, although at times it parallels the melody closely and adds rapid runs and arpeggios when the melody has a sustained note. Notice how the piccolo solo sketches the outline of the basic chords of the trio. Obbligato parts are generally played by piccolos, flutes, and clarinets in unison or octaves. This piccolo solo is featured the second and third times the trio is played.

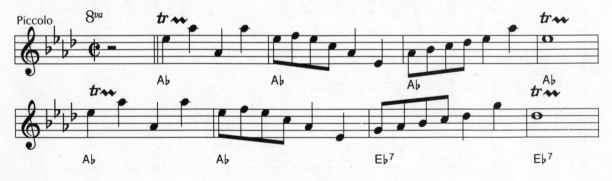

ILLUSTRATION 3

The trombones, meanwhile, play the *countermelody* on the third playing of the trio (Illustration 4). The entire section stands, slides flashing, roaring a grand *fortissimo*. The effect is strong and vigorous; however, the melody is not very satisfactory if played by itself. This is why it is a countermelody.

ILLUSTRATION 4

Before we go on to the rest of the band, let's line our three parts up together, as in Illustration 5. Arrows drawn on the score indicate the downbeats and upbeats.

ILLUSTRATION 5

Notice that on almost every downbeat *and* upbeat, one of the three parts starts a note. The effect of this is twofold: One, it reinforces the rhythmic drive of the march as a whole, with something constantly propelling the work forward; two, it helps to keep the three parts distinct from each other in the ear of the listener.

While all these things are going on, the tubas and French horns have the parts indicated in Illustration 6. These parts have two functions. First, they provide the basic

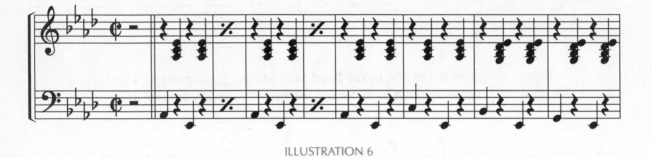

ILLUSTRATION 6

chords against which the other parts are set. Second, they help carry the background rhythm along, emphasizing the "one-two" beat that is so necessary for march music. In other words, these instruments are both chordal and rhythmic in function. They must play with the percussion section precisely, yet they must also stay in tune with the flutes, cornets, trombones, and so on.

Finally, let's examine the percussion section's part, which is sketched in Illustration 7. These parts reinforce the tuba and French horn parts rhythmically. The crisp

ILLUSTRATION 7

taps or thunderous rolls of the snares, and the steady thump of the bass drum, give a necessary drive to the music. This drive lightens the miles for marching feet. Add the splash of cymbals as a special effect, and you have a sound that thrills parade-watchers the world around.

Most traditional parade marches contain these same five functions: melody, obbligato, countermelody, rhythmic harmony, and special effects. Occasionally, as when the low brass are given the melody, there may be no countermelody or obbligato part, and the upper winds may join in the rhythmic harmony. Other variations on the basic plan may be heard at times as well. Most marches, however, stay true to the pattern outlined above.

Let's take the block-scored arrangement of "America, the Beautiful," used earlier, and adapt it to march style to see how the various parts may be created. The melody, of course, will go to the cornets, doubled by the alto saxophones and, an octave lower, by the tenor saxophones and baritone horn; we can keep the block-scored harmonization of the cornet parts (Illustration 8). The obbligato goes to the

ILLUSTRATION 8

flutes and clarinets; it follows the basic melody closely, but adds extra notes and runs for effect (Illustration 9). The trombones get the countermelody. Here they begin on a

ILLUSTRATION 9

rhythmically weak beat, outline the chord going up, and connect chord tones with passing tones coming down. Notice how the down- and upbeats are filled in by these three parts (Illustration 10). French horns and tubas sketch the harmony in rhythm

ILLUSTRATION 10

(Illustration 11). To avoid monotony, and to weaken the second beat somewhat, the tuba plays different notes, usually tonic and dominant, on each pair of beats. Usually, the second note is lower than the first. Finally, the percussion part (Illustration 12) reinforces the beat and adds some rhythmic interest of its own.

What about string parts? After all, marches can be played by orchestras, too. The violin is the basic melodic instrument in the orchestra; first and second violins would probably play the top two cornet parts an octave higher. The viola might be assigned to play the third cornet part; otherwise, it would be assigned the harmonic rhythm

ILLUSTRATION 11

ILLUSTRATION 12

part, along with the French horns. The cellos could be given the countermelody. This would allow the option of having the trombones join either the cornets in block harmony or the French horns in harmonic rhythm. Basses would take the part of the tuba, often *pizzicato* (plucked) in soft passages, *arco* (bowed) in loud. Winds would play the same general parts as in band, with trumpets instead of cornets. The percussion is, of course, essentially unchanged. With these comments as guides, you should be able to complete an arrangement of the piece for orchestra.

There are many other styles of composition you may wish to attempt, such as potpourri overtures with melodies from musicals, suites, fugues, tone poems, or symphonies—discussion of all these types lies far beyond the scope of this text. With some guidance from your teacher, you might wish to try writing something in one of these forms. Whatever sort of arranging you choose to do, keep the following points in mind:

1.  Music tends to be scored in SATB choirs of like instruments most of the time: Clarinet choir, all the woodwinds, all the brass, the saxophones, the horns, trumpets and baritone, trombones and tuba, and the full string section (with or without basses) are examples of such choirs. These choirs may be contrasted with the sound of the full ensemble, or with lightly scored parts for solo instruments with accompaniment.

2.  Most young arrangers over-score, keeping every instrument busy all the time. Strive for variety in tone color, in register (bass vs. treble), in dynamics, and in density of instrumentation (full ensemble vs. choir, or ensemble vs. solo). Listen to well-written music, and study the techniques that a good composer or arranger uses to achieve variety.

3. When switching from full ensemble to choir, or from choir to choir, it may be more effective to have one group begin before another ends. Again, variety is the key.

4. Carefully consider the character of the piece you are writing. If it is light and airy, keep the scoring light, with flutes, oboes, and clarinets prominent. If the mood is dark and somber, saxophones, French horns, and trombones may do the "speaking." If you are arranging a song with a text, take the text into consideration, verse by verse, in your setting. Illustrate the mood with proper instrumentation.

5. Learn how different instruments sound when played together, either in unison or in octaves. Common unison doublings include cornet with oboe, clarinet, or alto saxophone; baritone with tenor saxophone or bassoon; violin with flute; viola and/or cello with French horns; French horns with trombones and/or saxophones; and string bass with tuba. Octave, or double-octave, pairings often add a new color to the basic sound. Common examples are flute and trumpet, cornet with baritone or trombone, clarinet with tenor saxophone, violin with cello, 1st and 2nd violins in octaves, string bass with cello, and baritone with tuba. Listen carefully and study full instrumental scores to learn other effects of combining instruments.

6. It is also useful to learn which sounds can be substituted for others without doing too much violence to the original intentions of the composer. Groups lacking oboes, for instance, may substitute an alto saxophone or a cornet with a straight mute for the oboe solo.

Arranging for instruments is interesting, exciting, and offers limitless possibilities for the clever musician. As always, a good eraser may be your best friend, but don't be afraid to try outlandish things; how else will you learn how they sound? Write carefully, keeping especially aware of making accurate part transpositions. Try the standard ways of doing things, and then try some less conventional ideas of your own. Few thrills in the world are greater than hearing a big ensemble play music that YOU wrote or arranged, especially when it turns out well.

For further instruction in arranging music for instrumental ensembles, you may wish to consult the following books: *Music Arranging and Orchestration*, by John Cacavas, Melville, NY: Belwin-Mills Publishing Corp., 1975; and *The Technique of Orchestration*, by Kent Kennan, 2nd ed., Englewood Cliffs, NJ: Prentice-Hall, Inc., 1970.

# Instrument Ranges, Transpositions, and Descriptions

## *Woodwinds*

**Piccolo**

Written range:

Transposition:  Sounds an octave higher than written.

Usually plays above the treble register. Most effective in its second and third octave (from the bottom), where it has a cutting, sometimes shrill, sound.

**Flute**

Written range:

Sounds as written; no transposition.

Lowest octave is quite soft, but mellow and full when featured. Upper range clear, pure. Often doubles clarinets an octave higher.

**Oboe**

Written range:

Sounds as written.

Tone somewhat hoarse in lowest register, singing but nasal in the middle, tends to thin out and sound pinched on the highest notes.

**English Horn**

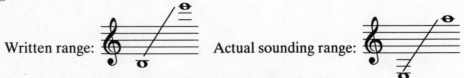

Written range:                        Actual sounding range:

Transposition:  Sounds a perfect fifth below the written note.

Tone is dark and resonant in the lowest register; nasal and a bit breathy in the middle; similar to oboe in high register. Low register is the most colorful.

### E-flat Clarinet

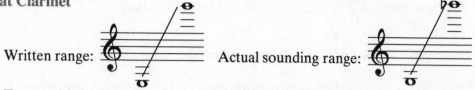

Written range:            Actual sounding range:

Transposition:  Sounds a minor third above the written note.

Tone is like the B-flat clarinet's. Most effective as a means of extending the clarinet tone quality above the treble register. Extremely high notes apt to be shrill and out of tune.

### B-flat Clarinet

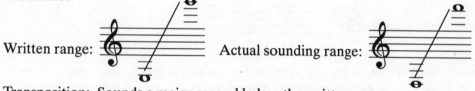

Written range:            Actual sounding range:

Transposition:  Sounds a major second below the written note.

The clarinet has the widest range of any band instrument. Lowest notes sound rich and woody; middle register notes are brilliant and clear, while top register notes (above written D above staff) become shrill and out of tune unless very carefully played. The clarinet is capable of both great agility and expressive lyricism. It can play wide jumps or arpeggiated parts easily.

### E-flat Alto Clarinet

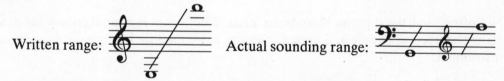

Written range:            Actual sounding range:

Transposition:  Sounds a major sixth below the written note.

While the alto clarinet's range is similar to the B-flat clarinet's, it is most effective in its lower register. The lower notes add a rich, alto-voice sonority to the basic clarinet sound. The higher notes sound like a heavy, somewhat wheezy B-flat clarinet.

### B-flat Bass Clarinet

Written range: 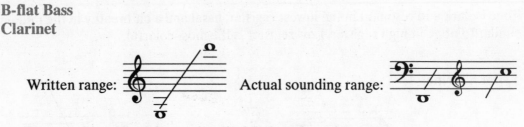 Actual sounding range:

Transposition: Sounds a major ninth below the written note.

Like the alto clarinet, the bass is most effective in its bottom notes, which have a woody, somewhat cello-like resonance.

### E-flat Contra-alto and B-flat Contra-bass Clarinets

Written range:

Actual sounding ranges are the same as for the alto and bass clarinets, except an octave lower. These two instruments extend the clarinet sound down below the bass register.

### B-flat Soprano Saxophone

Written range: 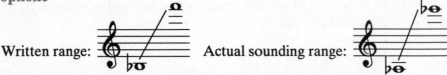 Actual sounding range:

Transposition: Sounds a major second below the written note.

Not often used, the soprano saxophone tends to be brassy in sound. Its low notes are rather hoarse; the middle and upper notes are more mellow. It is not a standard band instrument.

### E-flat Alto Saxophone

Written range: Actual sounding range:

Transposition: Sounds a major sixth below the written note.

The alto saxophone has a mellow, lyric sound, rather like a human voice. As with all the saxophones, the bottom notes are apt to sound rough and coarse.

### B-flat Tenor Saxophone

Written range: 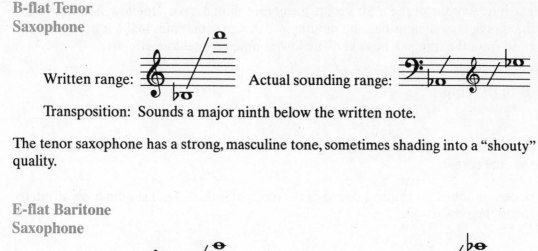 Actual sounding range:

Transposition: Sounds a major ninth below the written note.

The tenor saxophone has a strong, masculine tone, sometimes shading into a "shouty" quality.

### E-flat Baritone Saxophone

Written range: Actual sounding range:

Transposition: Sounds an octave and a major sixth below the written note.

While its upper notes sound rather thin, the lower octave has a strong, rough "cat's-tongue" quality. The sturdy bass of the saxophone choir, the baritone saxophone carries its reedy quality to the lower bass register.

### Bassoon

Written range:

Sounds the written pitches; no transposition.

Dryly expressive, the bassoon paints many moods, from somber to playful, sad to comical. Its lowest notes are rough-toned; the middle notes have a quality of plaintive-ness; the topmost notes are dry and pinched.

## *Brass*

### B-flat Cornet

Written range: 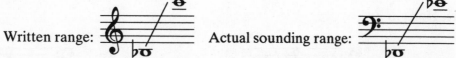 Actual sounding range:

Transposition: Sounds a major second below the written note.

The lyric soprano of the brass group, the cornet should have a mellow, liquid sound; changes in bore dimensions and mouthpiece design sometimes make it hard to distinguish from the trumpet, however. The lowest notes are seldom effective.

### B-flat Trumpet

Written range, actual sounding range, and transposition are identical to those of the cornet.

Brassy or noble, the brilliant sound of the trumpet is thrilling. It should have an edgier sound than the cornet.

### French Horn in F

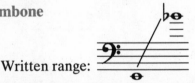

Written range:                    Actual sounding range:

Transposition:  Sounds a perfect fifth below the written note.

The haunting, distant tone of the French horn blends well with either brass or woodwind instruments. It has an extraordinary range for a brass instrument. Players usually specialize somewhat in their ranges; first and third parts usually have higher tones, while second and fourth have lower ones.

### Trombone

Written range:

Sounds the written pitches; no transposition.

The heroic tones of the trombone carry the trumpet's sonority into the tenor range. While most effective in its higher range, the trombone's lowest notes are powerful, especially when reinforcing the tuba.

### Baritone, Euphonium

Written range:

Sounds the written pitches; no transposition.

While usually considered to be interchangeable, these near-twins should sound as different as cornet and trumpet. The euphonium is bigger-toned and a bit darker in sound than the baritone. The sound of either is robust, not as edgy as the trombone's, and can be very lyric. **Note:** These parts may also be written in treble clef, as transposing instruments. Such parts are in B-flat, and the instrument sounds a major ninth below the written note.

## Tuba

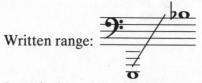

Written range:

Sounds the written pitches; no transposition.

While the tuba has a useful upper range for solo playing, its chief use as an ensemble instrument is to extend the brass quality below the bass register. The tone should be virile, but not edgy. The sousaphone is essentially the same instrument.

## *Percussion*

## Bell Lyre

Written range:

Actual sounding range is an octave higher.

The tone of the bell lyre is piercing, and carries well, which makes it most useful for marching groups. For concert use, the more refined glockenspiel is preferred.

## Glockenspiel
## or Orchestra Bells

Written ranges:

As you can see, ranges vary; the minimum range would be one and one half octaves. Like the bell lyre, the glockenspiel sounds an octave above the written pitch. Check the set for which you will be writing parts to determine its actual range.

**Note:** Unless indicated in the description, all percussion instruments, other than the above, sound the written pitch.

### Xylophone

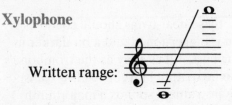

Written range:

Some xylophones do not have any notes below the lowest C; be sure to check this before writing parts for the instrument. The xylophone's sound is very dry and piercing, with no sustaining power unless the player rolls on a pitch. Rolls are indicated by slashes across the stem of a note, or above the note:

### Marimba

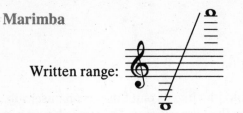

Written range:

The marimba's tone is mellower and more organ-like than the xylophone's. It is most effective in the lower octaves. A good player can play four-note chords; check out the technical facility of your player. The marimba is not effective in loud ensemble passages.

### Vibraphone

Written range:

"Vibes" have a pedal damper mechanism that allows them to play sustained notes or chords (pedal down) or shorter notes (pedal up). In addition, they have an electric motor that allows for a *vibrato* effect. The vibraphone is most effective in soft passages, or in small (especially jazz) ensembles.

### Chimes

Written range:

Transposition:  Chimes sound an octave below the indicated pitch.

Three types of chimes are found: one-octave sets, one-and-one-half octave sets, and two-octave sets. Check yours before writing parts for them. Chimes have limited uses, but are essential for those uses. Rapid note changes are difficult and generally not effective.

### Timpani

Written range:

The boom and thunder of timpani are inimitable colors in the ensemble. The instruments are difficult to adjust quickly to new pitches, so usually the timpani parts call for only two notes in lengthy sections of a piece. If the ensemble possesses three or four timpani, of course, other notes may be added. Different tone qualities are obtained by the use of mallets of varying hardness.

## Strings

### Violin

Written range:

All notes in the violin's range are useful melodically, though intonation problems are often acute in the highest notes. If you are not familiar with special playing techniques, such as *pizzicato*, *col legno*, *detaché*, or double stops, or with bowing markings, get help from your teacher or a string player. Violin parts are usually divided into 1sts and 2nds. **Note:** All string instruments play the notes actually written, except for the string bass, which sounds an octave below the written note.

### Viola

Written range:

The viola is seldom used as a solo instrument. Note the unusual (C) clef. The third line of the viola's staff corresponds to middle C of the grand staff: 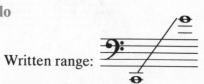.

### Cello

Written range:

Equally effective as either the bass voice of the string quartet (Violin I, Violin II, Viola, Cello) or as tenor-baritone melody voice in the string choir or full orchestra, the cello excels in lyric lines.

**Double Bass**

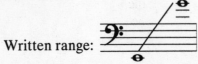

Written range:

All notes sound an octave lower than written. Seldom a melodic voice, the double bass either reinforces the cello an octave lower, or plays the bass voice line in the orchestra. In its lowest register, which is its most effective, it has a somewhat stuffy, unresonant tone. Some basses have a special mechanism that allows them to reach notes below E.

## Keys and Key Signatures

*(continued)*

G-flat

C-flat

F-sharp

C-sharp

# Appendix C:
## Arranging for Stage Bands and Rock Groups

Within this appendix, we will be describing writing techniques for specialized groups of instruments. These techniques make use of musical syntaxes and grammars appropriate to jazz and rock. All the comments found in the appendix on instrumental tone colors and ranges apply equally to the content of this appendix. If you have not mastered this information yet, you should first read through Appendix B.

## Definitions: Similarities, Differences

Stage bands are modern descendents of the enormously popular swing bands of the 1930's and 1940's. The style of music they play, loosely called big band jazz, evolved out of African American music that became popular in the early 1900's. Modern rock groups, on the other hand, evolved out of the rock and roll singers and bands of the early 1950's (Chuck Berry, Elvis Presley, and Jerry Lee Lewis, for example). These, in turn, had their roots in the same African American music as jazz.

These two styles of music have several things in common. For one thing, both have their roots in the blues. The twelve-measure blues form, with its characteristic chord progression (I-I-I-I-IV-IV-I-I-V-IV-I-I), is often heard in both. So is the *blues scale*, with its distinctive *blue notes* (lowered 3 and 7 in the major scale) that are usually harmonized by major chords, as in Illustration 1. Both styles also use scooped attacks of notes in which the performer slides up to the note instead of beginning exactly on pitch.

ILLUSTRATION 1

Two other common characteristics appear frequently. One is the prevailing use of syncopation to create a powerful rhythmic drive. The other is the use of solo improvisation. Both these characteristics also derive from African and African American music.

So much for the similarities. Jazz and rock have a number of distinguishing features as well, though they are blurred in the hybrid form known as *jazz-rock*. Of course, there are many styles of both jazz and rock, so generalities may not hold up in individual cases. What characteristics are shared between the music of the Preservation Hall Jazz Band and the free-form jazz of Ornette Coleman, or between Little Richard's rock and the sounds of *Yes* or *Kansas*? Nonetheless, certain general remarks apply to both jazz and rock, with the understanding that exceptions may be legion.

## Stage Bands

One common jazz feature is *swing rhythm*, which is a triplet interpretation of rhythmic figures. The figure written in Illustration 2A, for example, should automatically be played as in Illustration 2B, thereby making the rhythm pattern swing. Similarly, the pattern in Illustration 2C should be played as in Illustration 2D. The drummer in a jazz group often plays a rhythm on the ride cymbal that is notated as in Illustration 2E but played as in Illustration 2F.

ILLUSTRATIONS 2A, 2B, 2C, 2D, 2E, and 2F

Another stage band characteristic is that the harmony is dissonant, closely scored, and sometimes quite nontraditional. Chords with four or more tones—triads with added sixths, sevenths, ninths, or elevenths, and so on—provide the basic texture. Often, all the parts are crowded into the space of one octave, as in Illustration 3. When all the parts are kept so close to one another, chord progressions by fourths and fifths become difficult to use, even with extensive inversion. Instead of using the traditional principles of harmonization, therefore, a modified type of harmony is used. While the more important chords can be analyzed in a traditional fashion, what happens between these basic chords may look pretty strange at first sight.

ILLUSTRATION 3

Study Illustration 4 carefully; it's a jazz arrangement for five saxophones of the familiar song, "I've Been Working on the Railroad" (all parts in concert pitch). The chords from the original song are given in Roman numerals to help you orient yourself within the arrangement. As you can see, the first measure's chord is indeed the I chord, with an added sixth to provide the close, dissonant harmony that is so important in the stage band sound. In measure 3, also, the chord is a I with an added sixth. In measure 5, the chord is a IV with an added sixth, and in measure 7 it is a I with an added seventh for variety. So far, things look pretty conventional.

Measures 2, 4, and 6, however, don't follow the rules of traditional harmony or voice movement. Each measure presents a different, yet typical, technique of stage band harmonization. In measure 2, one could well keep the I chord sounding throughout, but doing so would sound quite static, and the piece would lack the vitality and drive that good stage band music should have. Instead, this arrangement uses a jazz progression that has become a cliché—$ii^7$, followed by a lowered $ii^7$, leading to a $I^6$ or $I^7$. The melody note (F) in the second beat of measure 2 doesn't fit the chord, but because it is on a weak beat, and because of the overall level of dissonance, it slides past without being noticed. Similarly, the melody note (C) in the fourth chord of the measure grates against the bass's C-flat if you hold the chord out, but it moves so quickly in the piece that it goes unremarked.

In measure 4 another trick of harmonization appears in which bass and soprano move in contrary motion from a unison or octave. If you analyze the harmony in measure 4, it makes no sense as a chord progression. In fact, the chords themselves are unimportant; you simply write the soprano and bass, and then fill in with musical stuffing made of notes between these two parts. Almost any notes, short of all minor seconds, will do nicely.

Measure 6 has a more traditional chord progression—$ii^7, V^{\flat 9}_7, I^7$ (which ties over to measure 7). The flatted ninth in the V chord adds a nice pungent spice to the chord, and it leads well to the similar dissonance of the $I^7$. Since the melody note in the $I^7$ is the third, the use of a $I^7$ chord works well. If the melody note had been the tonic, the seventh might have been too sharply dissonant to use.

One parting word about this example: The score you see here is typical of saxophone choir scoring for stage band. The top note of each chord is given to the first alto sax; the next highest is given to a tenor sax; the third highest to the other alto sax; the fourth highest to the other tenor sax; and the bottom note of the chord, of course, to

ILLUSTRATION 4

the baritone sax. Arranged in this way, as in Illustration 5, the sax section has a tight, closely woven sound.

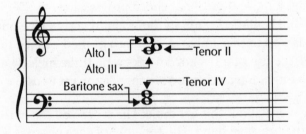

ILLUSTRATION 5

Such closely spaced harmonization is used for all instruments. The four trumpets or trombones each play a different pitch in each chord, with a minimum of doubling. When all the brass instruments play together, the trombones usually duplicate the trumpet notes at an octave lower.

There are a number of special jazz effects that are commonly used, and that add a great deal to the special flavor of jazz compositions. One such effect is the use of a wide range of mutes and other tone modifiers. Straight (sometimes written *strate*), cup, Solotone, Harmon, and wa-wa mutes are quite common. A plunger (which, in its simplest form, is the business end of a "plumber's helper") is sometimes called for. Using special flock-lined "hats" allows the arranger to achieve some lovely French horn effects, or the "doo-wah" figures that became a trademark of the Glenn Miller band (listen to a recording of "Tuxedo Junction" for this effect). When scoring parts for the hats, write the symbols ⊕ (for "in the hat") and ○ (for "open") above the notes, as in Illustration 6.

ILLUSTRATION 6

In many stage band compositions, the brass and the saxophones often play different roles. When the brass have the melody, as in Illustrations 7A and 7B, the saxes may have some sort of countermelody. When the saxes have the melody, the brass often punctuate with short rhythmic notes or phrases, as in Illustrations 7C and 7D. At still other times, of course, the two groups play the same material together. Study stage band scores to see how published arrangers handle the different sections of the ensemble throughout a piece.

Other jazz effects, such as smears, shakes, falls, and "doits," are indicated at the end of this chapter, with descriptions of how each is to be played. Again, listen to professional band recordings and study scores to get a feel for how and when these effects are used.

The typical stage band score has a separate line for each instrument. In order, from top to bottom, they are 1st Sax (alto), 2nd Sax (tenor), 3rd Sax (alto), 4th Sax (tenor), and 5th Sax (baritone). Next come four lines of trumpets, then four more for trombones, then lines for guitar, bass, drums, and piano. Among the trumpets and trombones, the first player takes the highest note of the chord, the second player the next highest, and so on. Parts may be written out on the score in either transposed form or in concert pitch, at the arranger's discretion. If you work out a condensed score in concert pitch in advance, you may write the parts on the master score in their transposed versions, which makes copying parts for individual instruments much easier.

ILLUSTRATIONS 7A, 7B, 7C, and 7D

Piano parts are usually just chord indications, with slashes on the bars to indicate the number of beats per measure. However, certain parts that the arranger wants played for special effects may be written out, as in Illustration 8A. A similar procedure is used for guitar, as in Illustration 8B. The electric guitar is written an octave above the sounding pitch. Unless a specific rhythm or special percussion part is desired, drum parts may be written as shown in Illustrations 8C and 8D. The drummer will be expected to fill out the part appropriately.

ILLUSTRATIONS 8A, 8B, 8C, and 8D

Most arrangements and compositions for stage band follow a typical structure that is similar to the following: introduction—chorus of piece played by entire group—optional repeat of first chorus, saxes playing the melody with brass figures—series of solo choruses, some with optional background riffs by sections—final ensemble chorus—coda. A *riff* is a repeated melodic and rhythmic figure that accompanies the featured melody. In Illustration 9, the saxophones play the melody while the trumpets play a riff accompaniment.

Variations on this basic formula are common, but usually minor. Sometimes an ensemble chorus (one chorus is a statement of the full melody) is placed in the middle of the piece. Soloists may play only a half chorus each; a trumpet may solo to the middle of the chorus and a tenor sax may finish the chorus, for example. If the arrangement goes on for two minutes or more, the final chorus may be in a new key to provide some variety. If you have several strong soloists, you may give them four-measure solos in fixed rotation—swapping fours, as it is called.

A brief note about bass parts is needed. For pure jazz writing, keep the bass solidly on the beat, either two or four notes per measure. When writing bass parts on each beat, consider using a *walking bass* in which the bass player has a different note on each beat. The first and third notes of such patterns should be notes of the basic triad, or perhaps the seventh, but the second and fourth notes can be passing tones or other pitches. For jazz-rock bass parts, use an active, syncopated bass as you would when writing for a rock group.

ILLUSTRATION 9

# Rock Groups

Rock music also has certain typical characteristics. Rock's basic approach to rhythm contrasts with swing rhythm; it is usually a heavy, "1-and-2-and" beat, or alternatively a pounding "1-**2**-3-**4**" pattern, with strong emphasis on 2 and 4. Once in a while, especially in 1950's rock and roll, a loping rhythm-and-blues $\frac{12}{8}$ meter is used, but the feel here is all for the downbeat, rather than the offbeat as in swing. Illustration 10 shows a rock triplet pattern. In rock music, every downbeat and every upbeat may be marked by either the bass, the melody, or some other part, much as in the military march discussed in Appendix B. In Illustration 11 almost every possible down-

ILLUSTRATION 10

beat and upbeat is reinforced by a note in the arrangement that begins on that part of the beat.

ILLUSTRATION 11

The harmonies of rock are usually much less complex than those of jazz, but the relationships of chords and the voicing are often quite nontraditional. Rock and roll songs often contain only three or four simple chords, such as I, IV, V, and vi, and frequently there is parallel motion between chords. Progressions of a whole step up or down are common, and modal scales, as in the Beatles' "Eleanor Rigby," may be used. Jazz improvisations are usually done on a sequence of chords; in rock, on the other hand, improvisations are usually backed up by an *ostinato*. This is a repeated pattern of notes, often in the bass, of two or four measures in length, perhaps with chords included. Illustration 12 shows two typical bass ostinatos for lead guitar solos.

Rock music is played largely by electronic or electronically amplified instruments: electric guitar, electric bass, electric piano, synthesizer, perhaps drum machine, and other optional plug-in instruments. Aside from the drum set, which seldom needs (but still may have) amplification, all the rest of the group is usually wired for sound. There are few transpositions for rock groups; guitar and electric bass are both written

ILLUSTRATION 12

an octave higher than they sound, but all other instruments play actual pitches, unless you add such instruments as saxophones or trumpets.

The typical structure of a rock composition is similar to that of a jazz work: introduction—ensemble chorus—optional ensemble repeat—optional improvisation over an ostinato—ensemble chorus—coda. The improvisation is *not* based on the original melody but is a free creation set over the ostinato. The coda may be a "tape-loop" phrase that repeats over and over, as in the Beatles tune "Hey, Jude."

Harmonically, rock is apt to be mostly triadic, with much parallel motion by steps or by thirds. One reason is the ease of moving from one chord to another on guitar by simply sliding the fingers up or down the neck a few frets. Frequent modulations within a chorus are common, and some chord changes are quite nontraditional (i.e., C major to A major). Voices are much more important in rock than in jazz. Not only are most rock instruments amplified, but their tones can be altered electronically. *Reverb* effects are occasionally used, as is the *cry-baby* foot pedal attachment. Fuzz-tone effects are sometimes used on electric guitars or basses. Synthesizers, of course, can produce a nearly infinite variety of sounds. It is beyond the scope of this book to detail the possible tone modifications available to rock ensembles. Find out what equipment is available to the performers for whom you will be writing, and explore its possibilities. Then try writing material for the group, and revise as needed.

This is only a brief sketch of how to write music for stage bands and rock groups. For further instruction, consult this book: *Modern Arranging Technique*, by Gordon Delamont, Delevan, NY: Kendor Music, Inc., latest edition. Delamont's book is clearly written and covers many different styles, with good and helpful suggestions in every part.

## Special Jazz Effects

| | |
|---|---|
| | ***Smear.*** Slide upward (on the trombone) from the lower to the higher note over the duration of the first note. Can also be a chromatic or diatonic scale on other instruments. |
| | ***Spill or fall.*** Play the first note solidly, then run (or slide) rapidly downward the approximate interval indicated by the wiggly line. |
| | ***Shake.*** Shake the brass instrument violently while playing the note. The pitch should vary upward. |
| | ***Doit*** (pronounced "DOYT"). Play the note, then (on brass instruments) lip the pitch upward sharply while pressing valves halfway down. |
| | ***Gliss (upward).*** On a brass instrument, press valves halfway down, begin low, lip the pitch upwards and gradually release valves until you reach the indicated note. Woodwinds play scalar or chromatic runs. Glisses can be short or long. |
| | ***Gliss (downward).*** Attack the note, then half-valve (on brass instruments) and lip downward. Woodwinds play scale runs downward. |
| | ***Plop.*** Rapid lip slide or scale run from an indefinite high pitch to the indicated note. |
| | ***Flip.*** This is a brass instrument figure. Attack the first note, then lip the pitch upward rapidly, then immediately back down to the second indicated note. |

# Appendix D:
# Suggested Recordings to
# Use with This Book

Bach, J. S., "Contrapunktus VII" from *The Art of the Fugue*—CBS M2K-42270; "'Little' Fugue in G Minor"—Col MS6261

Bartók, *Concerto for Orchestra*, 2nd Mvt.—Merc 432017-2PM; *Mikrokosmos*, Nos. 37, 48, 55, 56, 58, 62, 63—same

Beethoven, *Sonata Pathétique*, 1st Mvt.—Jubilee JL41013; *Symphony No. 5*—Telarc Stereo DG 10060

Brahms, *Intermezzo in A*, Op. 118, No. 2—LaserLight 15-052; *Symphony No. 1*, 3rd Mvt.—RCA LSC-2711

Chopin, *Prélude No. 4*—MusHer MHS 1841

Copland, "Fanfare for the Common Man"—Pro Arte CDD-102

Debussy, "Clouds" from *Nocturnes*—London 414040-2LH; *Syrinx*—RCA RCD1-7173

Dvořák, *Symphony No. 9*, 4th Mvt.—Quintessence 3 Pc 3703

Handel, "He Was Despised" from *Messiah*—Col M2S 607

Haydn, *String Quartet* Op. 76, No. 3—Denon C37-7094

Joplin, "Entertainer Rag"—Quintessence CDQ 2019

Liszt, *Les Préludes*—CBS CD MYK 37772

Milhaud, "Copacabana," *Saudades do Brasil*—PCD 846

Mozart, *Eine Kleine Nachtmusik*—London STS 15506; *Symphony No. 40*, 1st Mvt.—Nonesuch H=71047

Offenbach, "Barcarolle" from *Tales of Hoffmann*—Chesky CD 61

Purcell, "Dido's Lament" from *Dido and Aeneas*—Etcetera KTC-1064

Schumann, *Papillons*—Centaur CRC-2065

Tchaikovsky, *Romeo and Juliet*—Quintessence CDQ 2023; *Symphony No. 3*, 5th Mvt.—Quintessence 3 pc 3701

Vivaldi, *Concerto Grosso in D Minor* Op. 3, No. 11—Angel CDD-63888

# Index